II

MCKEAN COUNTY MURDERS

&

Mysterious Deaths

Volume I

By James T. Baumgratz

Copyright © 2020 by James T. Baumgratz

Printed in the United States of America

ISBN: 978-0-9708236-4-9

First Printing: November 2020

All rights reserved. No part of this book may be reproduced or transmitted in any form or by any means, electronic or mechanical, including photocopying, recording, or by any information storage and retrieval system without written permission from the author, except for the inclusion of brief quotations in a review

Published by:

Baumgratz Publishing, LLC
P.O. Box 100
Ridgway, PA 15853

For the late Edward "Pete" Anderson, a great entrepreneur who encouraged me to "write, write and write some more." You will always be an inspiration.

CONTENTS

1. Forbidden Love - Smethport — 1
2. Blackout - Crosby — 16
3. Scandalous – Tuna Valley — 21
4. Double Jeopardy - Kane — 26
5. You Belong to Me – Port Allegany — 50
6. Tarport — 54
7. Death in Clermont — 67
8. A Clear Case of Suicide - Bradford — 75
9. Double-Crossed – Bradford — 88
10. A Friendly Game of Poker – Lewis Run — 94
11. Mistaken Identity – Cady Hollow & Keating — 99
12. The Inheritance - Bradford — 106
13. The Assyrian Peddlers - Clermont — 119
14. Pig Island - Bradford — 128
15. The Saga of Francis Godino – Corryville — 135
16. The Brewer House – Mt. Jewett — 150

CONTENTS

17.	Feeble-Minded - Bradford	155
18.	Death at Kinzua	163
19.	Rubbed Out - Bradford	169
20.	Major Ashton - Bradford	175
21.	Dementia - Smethport	182
22.	Madness – Port Allegany	187
23.	Missing in Ludlow	192
24.	Westline	199
25.	In Defense of Her Honor - Olivedale	213

FROM THE AUTHOR

In this, the first volume of McKean County Murders, I explore over 25 cases from the county's past. I have researched well over 100 murders and mysterious deaths in McKean County and these historical crimes are truly something that should be of interest to all.

The innocent victims of these homicides should never be forgotten. I will be placing flowers on each victim's grave I discover, as a sign that their tragic lives have not been forgotten.

In my prior books on Elk County, I found that alcohol played a large part in many homicides that took place in that county. I did not find such a common denominator in McKean County however bootlegging did figure in many of the deaths.

I hope you enjoy this first volume of McKean County Murders & Mysterious Deaths. Look for more McKean County and Potter County books in process. Updates are published on my Facebook pages.

MCKEAN COUNTY MURDERS

&

Mysterious Deaths

Volume I

Cover Photo: Miss Anna Peeler

Forbidden Love

The grave of Mary Reilly located in St. Elizabeth's Cemetery in Smethport.

Forbidden love is one of the most common causes of homicidal violence in the human race. The victim is often the parent or person who forbids the romance from taking place, and they are murdered as they are seen as standing in the way of the romance. In this case, the victim was the object of one man's twisted desires, and although she and her family believed she was safe from any harm, they were proved to have been dead wrong. This case also resulted in the second hanging in McKean County, and it would be fourteen years before this supreme penalty would be used again.

Andrew Tracy was a young and upcoming lawyer in Smethport in the latter half of the 19th century. His law practice was centered on real estate and license procurement, and by all accounts, he had a small but steady clientele. Tracy was unmarried and would often be found carousing the local establishments and imbibing in his favorite drink, whiskey. Andrew was looking for a lifelong mate to marry and believed he had found one in his beautiful first cousin, Mary Reilly. Mary, not yet eighteen when Tracy began to court her, was smitten with his attentions and looked forward to every visit Tracy made to her father's house. Mr. Andrew Reilly, father of Mary, did not catch on right away to the blossoming romance taking place under his roof. When he finally discovered the relationship, he was horrified. Mr. Reilly, a strict Catholic, knew that the church and indeed the state looked upon relationships between first cousins as an abomination and set forth to break up this relationship at all costs. Tracy had already asked Mary to marry him, and in the young couples' eyes, they were betrothed. Mr. Andrew Reilly called the Squire Tracy to his house. In front of his daughter, he told Tracy in no uncertain terms that he objected to any type of relationship between Tracy and his daughter, and he would resist it with his life if necessary. Tracy exploded in anger and ripped open his vest, exposing his chest. He put his hand on his heart and said, his life is nothing; you can kill me if you will. This incident happened in 1875. Mr. Reilly eventually settled Tracy down, but the seeds of discontent were sown. Whenever Mr. Reilly saw Tracy after this date, he eyed him with suspicion, and Tracy did the same. As the years passed, Tracy seemed to have gotten over his lust for Mary, and her father no longer worried about his daughter. Mary, quite beautiful and from a wealthy family, had begun to correspond with a gentleman who lived in Buffalo. She was observed by Tracy walking hand in hand with this man down Main Street of Smethport, much to his displeasure. Tracy, who never got over his infatuation with Mary, was incensed and soon his obsession with Mary would end both of their lives.

On September 18th, 1878, Mary Reilly, accompanied by her cousin Miss Belle Mullin, headed to the millinery (*women's hats*) store of Mary Tracy on Main Street. Mary Tracy was a sister of Andrew and often had get-togethers in her store. While the small crowd in the store chatted, Andrew came into the store accompanied by a cousin, Frank

McCabe. They chatted pleasantly with Mary Reilly, and then Andrew asked Mary to sing a song for him. Mary Reilly was known to have a beautiful voice, and she at once took up his suggestion and sat down at the organ to play one of her favorite songs. While Mary was singing and playing the organ, her father, Andrew Reilly, came into the store and paid Mary Tracy some money he owed on an account. He then went to Mary at the organ and handed her a letter she had received from her suitor in Buffalo. Tracy observed this exchange of the letter and at once became suspicious. Andrew Tracy then asked her to play "Catalina," and when she was halfway through the song, he walked out of the store with McCabe. Mary shouted "good night" to both of them, but Tracey did not turn around and acknowledge her salutation.

Mary sang several more songs and received applause from the small group who were present. At around 9 in the evening, Mary and her friend Belle decided to call it a night and headed out onto Main Street for the short walk up the street to the Mullin residence. Mary and Belle had been friends since their school days, and Mary had already made plans to spend the night at her friend's house. As the women reached the Hamlin Hardware Store, Mary remarked to Belle about the loud footsteps that could be heard following them. The two girls, arm in arm, quickened their pace, hoping to reach the Mullin residence before being overtaken. Just as the girls reached the gate to the Mullin house, a man appeared. A loud gunshot was heard, and Mary fell to the ground dragging her friend Belle as she collapsed. Belle saw a man of medium height run down Water Street and disappear. Belle did not recognize the man and thought that he had only shot the pistol at their heads to scare them. When she reached out to help her friend Mary up, she realized her hand was covered with blood, and she screamed. Her screams brought many neighbors out of their houses, and they carried the mortally wounded Mary into the Mullin residence. They all could see that she had suffered a bullet wound to the left temple and she was unconscious. Dr. Freeman was summoned, but after examining Mary, he found that there was nothing that could be done, and Mary expired from her wound several hours later, never regaining consciousness.

The murder of Mary Reilly sent shock waves through the ordinarily peaceful settlement. Sheriff King interviewed Belle and upon hearing her story of spending the evening at Mary Tracy's store; he interviewed everybody present in the store that evening in hopes of finding a clue as to the assailant. The only person who was at the store that night and who could not be located was Andrew Tracy. Sheriff King had already been informed of the failed romance between Tracy and Ms. Reilly, and he quickly became the prime suspect. Adding to his suspicion was that Tracy had seemingly fled the county, and when he interviewed Tracy's brother John, he knew he had the correct doubts. John told the sheriff that Tracy had visited him late that night and had confessed to having done something very wrong and John would hate him for it. He did not admit to John that he killed Mary, only that he had been slighted and was going away and would never be seen again. Sheriff King formed a posse and sent word to neighboring towns along the railroad to be on the lookout for Andrew Tracy, who was wanted for murder.

Word was received at Portville, New York, to be on the lookout for Andrew Tracy. Archie McDougall, the local constable, received the notice from Sheriff King to be on the lookout for a stranger from Smethport, and the message contained a description of Tracy. On September 20th, McDougall noticed two strangers walking along the sidewalk going in the direction of Olean. McDougall stepped up behind the man matching the description of Tracy and attempted to arrest him. Tracy threw his overcoat down and started to run. Tracy had a revolver in his hand as he ran, but McDougall was able to catch up with him and put his arms around his waist and tackled him. McDougall secured the pistol and told Tracy that if he did not cooperate, he would put handcuffs on him. Tracy said he would comply and accompanied McDougall to the post office. At the post office, Tracy was questioned as to whether he came from Smethport, and if his name was Andrew Tracy. Tracy answered in the affirmative and asked how long he was going to be detained. McDougall said that a young woman had been shot in Smethport, and he was the prime suspect. McDougall said he was trying to find out if he had the right man. Tracy said, "You needn't go to that," and waited until Sheriff King arrived to take him into custody and return him to Smethport. McDougall secured a revolver, two knives, and a pair of scissors from Tracy and turned these items over to King when he arrived. Tracy did not want to return to Smethport and attempted to resist when he was placed on the train. The sheriff calmed him down, and he went peacefully. An angry mob awaited Tracy at the Smethport train station with the intention of lynching the accused. Sheriff King had Tracy smuggled out of the back of the train into a waiting carriage, and Tracy was transported to the jail before the angry crowd knew he had escaped their wrath.

Mary Reilly was but twenty-three years of age when she met her demise. By all accounts, she was a very talented and beautiful young lady on the inside and outside. Her remains had lain in state at her father's house near Smethport. A large group of mourners turned out for her funeral, which was held in St. Elizabeth's Catholic Church. The remains of Mary were buried at the St. Elizabeth's Cemetery outside of the city.

A coroner's jury was formed and heard the accounts of numerous people as to their observations on that fateful night. Belle Mullin recounted how she had been walking back to her house when they heard loud footsteps, and a shot rang out. She could however not identify Tracy as the killer.

Dr. Freeman testified that he had attended Mary Reilly five minutes after she was shot. He found a bullet wound in her left temple and could find no other wound on the body. He said Mary had died about forty minutes after being shot.

John Tracy, the brother of Andrew, then testified that his brother had come to their house on the night of the shooting and told them he had done something horrible. Andrew brandished a pistol and told his family to tell anybody who came looking for him that he was not there that evening. John said Tracy had pointed his pistol at him and made him promise, which John did. John noted that Andrew appeared to have been intoxicated that evening and said his brother had a known addiction to liquor.

Several people testified as to seeing Andrew consume whiskey on the night of the murder. His friend, Frank McCabe, testified that he had been drinking with Andrew throughout the night, and both had gone into Mary Tracy's store. Mary Reilly was singing and playing different instruments, and after listening to several songs, the men retired to the porch. As McCabe and Andrew talked on the porch, Mary Reilly and Belle Mullin came out and crossed the street walking up Main Street. McCabe followed Andrew up the street, and both could see the young ladies walking further ahead. McCabe said he last saw Andrew cross the road towards the girls when the women were in front of Hamlin's store, close to the Mullin residence. He said he saw Andrew turn after crossing the street, and he was now directly behind the girls. McCabe said he went into the Bennett House and spoke with Charley Bluidbetty for a couple of minutes. Frank Richmond rushed into the house and said that Mary Reilly was shot. McCabe ran up the street and found Mary lying on the sidewalk in a dying condition. He said he saw no more of Andrew after that, but within a half-hour of the shooting, he began to suspect Andrew was the killer.

The coroner's jury then deliberated and came back with the verdict that on September 18th, Mary Reilly had come to her death by a gunshot fired at the hands of Andrew Tracy. Formal first-degree murder charges were then produced and served upon Tracy, a resident in the local jail. The penalty for a conviction of first-degree murder being death by hanging.

The trial of Andrew Tracy commenced on Monday, February 24th, 1879, at the Smethport Courthouse. Judge H. W. Williams presided with Judges Burnham and Brownell assisting. The case was prosecuted by District Attorney Smith, who was assisted by W. W. Brown of Bradford and M. F. Elliott of Wellsboro. The defense consisted of A. B. Richmond of Meadville, Colonel C. B. Curtis of Erie, and Edward

McSweeney of Smethport. The jury chosen included Lewis Holley, Ira Burdick, E. H. Holmes, T. H. Collins, Stephen Irons, William Foster, Charles Jones, George Wright, F. W. Fonda, Joseph Post, Gideon Davis, and Willis Ripley. Andrew Tracy pled "not guilty" to the charges, and the prosecution began their case. The prosecution and defense would call well over fifty witnesses, but only those with substance have been included here to streamline the case.

Ms. Belle Mullin was called and testified that she had spent the evening with Mary Reilly at Mary Tracy's store. Andrew Tracy was present intermittently that evening, coming in and out of the store. Belle thought that Andrew seemed restless that evening but that she did not have any conversation with him. She said that Mary had asked Andrew to play an accompaniment to her solo, and Andrew complied. Andrew had his head down most of the time he was in the store and barely made eye contact. Belle said that when she and Mary left, Andrew had already retired to the front porch, and Mary said goodnight to him as they passed. Ms. Mullin further testified about hearing the footsteps coming up behind them and the shot that rang out that resulted in her friend's death.

Dr. Freeman then testified about receiving the notice of the shooting of Mary Reilly on September 18th and attending her at the Mullin residence. Freeman said that Mary had suffered a gunshot wound to the left temple, and death took place within forty minutes of his arrival. He said he could not save her as there was too much damage to her brain. Dr. Freeman also testified as to knowing the defendant for many years and recalled a conversation he had with him the previous summer. Andrew had asked him where in the head would a gunshot be most fatal. Dr. Freeman said he showed Andrew the area of the temple which would be most lethal. Freeman never questioned Andrew why he wanted this information but noticed the wound on Mary was in the area that he had previously told Andrew was the most fatal.

Frank McCabe was called. He reiterated the story he told at the coroner's inquest and cemented his recollection that Andrew Tracy was last seen walking briskly behind Mary and Ms. Mullins shortly before the shooting.

Andrew Reilly, the father of Mary, was called, and he said he last saw his daughter alive around 7 o'clock on September 18th at Mary Tracy's store. He said he handed Mary a letter from her paramour but could not be sure if Andrew saw this. Reilly told of one day meeting Tracy in the company of his daughter on their farm several years past. He at that time forbade Tracy from courting his daughter as they were first cousins, and it was unchristian and against the rules of the Church. Tracy said his intentions were honorable to his daughter, but Mr. Reilly said this could never be. Reilly said he had never had any trouble with Tracy after that date until the tragic shooting. The prosecution then rested.

The defense then asked the judges to allow Andrew Tracy to change his plea from "not guilty" to "guilty of the killing by reason of insanity." District Attorney Smith objected to the changing of the plea. After a lengthy legal argument, the judges allowed the defendant to answer a series of questions in the courtroom. Upon the application of the defendant in open court, he was permitted to withdraw his plea of not guilty and to plead guilty by reason of insanity to the murder of Mary Reilly. This changing of his plea took his fate from the hands of the jury into the hands of the judges.

Defense Attorney Richmond then began his case by proposing to show that the defendant had no motive for the killing of Mary and that she was the dearest object to him on earth. He said the defendant had sustained a severe head injury from which he never fully recovered. His mental capacity was such that he could not be guilty of willful, deliberate, and premeditated murder.

Attorney Richmond introduced and read one of the love letters that Mary had written to the defendant to show how much his heart had been strained. It was noted that Mary had continued to write "love" letters to Tracy almost up to and including the week of her murder. The letter read: "I feel proud to think my love is essential to your happiness" wrote the young girl in February of 1876. "You will always have my love as long as I live to give it. You will ever be the one dear object of my affections and be enshrined in my heart until I return my soul to its maker. I can never tell you how I do love you and all I do to make you happy. I could go to the blackest forest and there live with you forever. I could be happy to be with you, even though there would be no one else near. I love you most passionately. I always think of you. Oh, how I long to show you how warm my feelings are for you."

James Tracy, a brother of Andrew, was called to testify. James said he noticed that Andrew was gloomy and melancholy and would often go and sit by himself. Andrew avoided company and preferred to be by himself and left their house whenever people visited. James said his brother had a revolver and had placed it against his head and pulled the trigger. The gun was not loaded, and James took the gun from his brother and locked it up in a bureau. Tracy said he often slept in the same bed as his brother (*common in those days due to space*) and noticed his brother often self-polluted (*masturbated*) during the night. In those days, masturbating was considered a sure sign of mental illness. He also said Andrew made strange and inappropriate trades with children, such as once trading an expensive and sharp double-bitted ax for a little magnet. Andrew also liked to show children the money he had about him and would hold the shiny coins up to the children every few minutes. Whenever Andrew saw a woman approach, he would turn and hurry the other way and avoided all contact with women excepting his mother and sisters.

Many other witnesses were called who described strange habits Andrew had, which included writing with his finger on walls and tables and books. These habits seemed more of a nervous habit than anything else. All who knew Andrew said he was of a peculiar type and never known to be sociable. Many of his friends said he had a penchant for drinking whiskey until he was intoxicated, and when drunk, he seemed to take more risks than usual. The defense then rested without calling the defendant to the stand.

District Attorney Smith now opened the argument for the prosecution while addressing the judges, as the jury was no longer tasked with the verdict. Smith compared Mary Reilly to the Virgin Mary and said her death was a deliberate action taken by a sane person, the defendant. The prosecutor said the defendant was not suffering from a secret vice, but rather his actions resulted from unrestrained and uncontrollable passion. This passion grew out of youthful precocity, the pampering of friends, and the knowledge on his part that he possessed talents uncommon to most youths. His prosecution of the case was not due to malice but solely for a sense of justice and duty. Smith asked the judges to carefully weigh the prosecution's evidence to determine the defendant's degree of guilt.

Assistant Prosecutor Brown then delivered his plea to the court. He informed the court that although he had a long-standing friendship with Father Michael Tracy, a brother of Andrew and a priest, he was not swayed by this friendship. Brown attacked the defense argument of insanity and said that the actions of Andrew were one of deliberate purpose and premeditation. He noted that Andrew planned and carried out the murder and his fleeing the scene of the crime proved he knew right from wrong. Attorney Brown also criticized the testimony of the defense regarding Andrew's mental state and said all of the testimony of the witnesses was trivial to the extreme. His final plea to the court was for justice in this case which would show that a human life has an additional safeguard thrown around it.

Attorney Richmond opened for the defense and stated the reason the defense had taken the verdict away from the jury and placed it in front of the court. He feared that the known consensus of the community against the prisoner would find its way into the jury box and have influence in the minds of the jurors in making their verdict. The attorney then spoke at length on this issue of insanity and about how insanity had been shown in the testimony for the defense. Richmond stated that the prosecution had not proven a motive for the murder and introduced several letters written by the deceased to the defendant, showing that her love for him had not waned despite their not being formally together. He read the last letter Mary had written to the defendant, only two weeks before the shooting where she had signed off "your own wife, Mary." He stated that what more proof of a trigger of insanity would be the unrequited love affair banned by the church and her family, and this would wreck and destroy the mind of any young man. Knowing how much love existed between the defendant and the deceased, what further proof of insanity could be produced than when he killed the one who was the dearest object to him that existed upon earth. Richmond concluded by pointing to the defendant's attempt to commit suicide, his frequent nighttime masturbation and sleeplessness, his writing with his fingers upon the walls and books and his lack of socialization as all proof of his insanity.

Colonel Curtis closed the defense by comparing the case of Cromwell in England as an attempt to control the mob as what was happening to Tracy. Curtis said that even though Cromwell had died a natural death, his body was taken from its coffin and hanged to satisfy the clamor of the mob. He further talked about the strange conduct and manner of the defendant, which he claimed could not be reconciled with the actions of one possessed of a sound mind. He described the affectionate relationship between the defendant and his victim and stated the murder was evidence of insanity as there was no other explanation plausible.

M. F. Elliott then gave the final speech for the prosecution. Elliott defended the community against the charge of mob rule, which the defense had compared them to. He ridiculed the position of the defense that the accused knew enough to murder in the second degree but not murder in the first degree. The prosecutor stated that the murder was indeed premeditated and that the actions of the defendant in fleeing the area after the murder was proof of such intent. He said that the love of Mary had changed at the time of the murder, as shown by her not embracing the defendant on that last night, but instead, she left the Tracy store and went on up the street instead of leaving with Andrew. The motive for this murder was forbidden love. He said the defense had not established the insanity of the defendant and that he was guilty of the charge of murder in the first degree and should face the ultimate consequences for his actions.

Upon the conclusion of Mr. Elliott's address, Judge Williams stated that he would consult a few moments with his colleagues to ascertain whether they agreed in their views as to the disposition of the case.

The three judges then consulted in an undertone, while the vast audience awaited the result of their deliberations with anticipation. During this time, Tracy sat as immovable as before, with downcast eyes, the only indication of the struggle going on within his breasts being his rapid winking.

After a lapse of precisely three minutes, Judge Williams delivered the verdict of the court, as follows:

"After consultation with my associates, I think we are substantially agreed as to the proper disposition to be made at present in this case. The fact of killing is admitted. This shifts the onus of the proof from the Commonwealth to the defendant. The defendant sets up as defense his insanity. The burden of proof is put upon him, and it becomes his duty to satisfy us of the existence of this insanity. The proof must be such that its weight firmly leads to the conclusion of the existence of such a mental condition as would reduce the grade of the offense. The existence of a reasonable doubt as to the sanity of the defendant is not enough. The fact must be established by the same sort of proof as would be necessary to establish the existence of any other fact in the case. The question for us, therefore, is whether the defendant has shown insanity to exist in this case. Does the weight of the testimony fairly lead to the conclusion that his condition of mind is such as to render him incapable of deliberate purpose necessary to constitute murder in the first-degree? The circumstances under which the crime was committed are very clearly shown on the part of the defendant. They show this purpose of having existed for some considerable time and worked out with persistence by the defendant. They further show the stealthy manner in which the offense was committed. They show flight. They show efforts at concealment. They are, therefore, presented as evidence of consciousness of the moral quality of this act. We cannot say that we regard the testimony on the part of the defendant as to his insanity as satisfactory to us upon that question. Yet, it will lead to the conclusion that the defendant is, and has been for a number of years, in a somewhat morbid state of mind. We are disposed of, therefore, in view of the evidence and the conclusions, we have now expressed as drawn from it, to find against the defendant on this question. But we do it with the understanding that our sentence shall be deferred until the April term in order to afford counsel for the defendant an opportunity to make an application to the Board of Pardons for commutation of the sentence from death to imprisonment for life. In this application, the court will heartfully join. We find the defendant, therefore, guilty of murder in the first-degree. The sentence will be postponed, as already indicated."

The attorneys for Tracy immediately filed an application with the Board of Pardons asking for his sentence to be commuted from death by hanging to a term of life imprisonment. The application included a letter asking for a commutation signed by Judge Williams and his associates. On September 26th, the application was denied, and a date for execution was set as being on October 9th. The governor then granted a respite, and another application was made to the pardon board to reconsider their decision. This application also included the Judge's letter as well as numerous letters questioning the unsoundness of the prisoner's mind and a large mass of additional evidence showing the irresponsibility of the defendant. The Board of Pardon once again refused the application, and a final appeal to the Supreme Court for a special writ of error was also refused. The execution was formally set for December 4th at the Smethport jail.

Tracy spent his final night on this earth in the company of his two brothers, who were catholic priests, and three other priests. He was resigned to his fate, although he had repeatedly and persistently stated that he should not be made to suffer for a crime born out of an impulse. Tracy wrote numerous letters to family and friends during his last night. Tracy also had written extensively criticizing the district attorney, who steadfastly opposed the commutation of his sentence, the governor who signed his death warrant, the father of his victim who had opposed his relationship with the deceased, and the Catholic Church for not giving him a special dispensation for the marriage. Tracy also wrote of the contempt he had for Thomas Carroll; whom Mary had written several love letters to. He condemned the newspapers of the day for what he considered their one-sided contempt for him. He also wrote another statement in which he asked his family to have his remains cremated and how his body was to be burned. He expressed his certainty that he would reach heaven, and there he would be able to write to his heart's desire.

Tracy's execution was to have been between 10 a.m. and 3 p.m. The event caused a stir when it was decided to be held at 1:30 in the afternoon, as most previous executions had taken place as close to 10 in the morning as possible. Tracy was led out of his cell at one-thirty and walked to the gallows accompanied by Father Dent and two other priests. He wore a black silk gown over his ordinary clothes and was seen to kiss a cross in his hand. After a few moments of prayer, the sheriff then made one final request of Tracy. "Andy Tracy, have you anything to say why the sentence of the law should not be passed upon you?" Tracy answered, "Nothing at all."

The sheriff then put the black hood over Tracy's head and adjusted the noose over his neck. As Tracy continued to recite prayers out loud, the sheriff cut the rope, and the body of Tracy fell like a rock onto the floor of the concrete corridor with a sickening thud. The knot that had been placed in the noose had given away, and although Tracy's neck was broken, he was very much alive. Tracy was paralyzed from the neck down and moaned as he lay upon the cold concrete. Two deputies immediately went to pick up the prisoner and had to physically carry him back up to the scaffold as he was unable to move any limb. Sheriff Sartwell *(who had replaced the retired Sheriff King)* then retied the knot on the noose, and the deputies held Tracy upright while the sheriff put the noose around him again and this time, when he cut the rope, the noose held, and Tracy expired after swinging for around ten minutes. It was noted that Tracy never said a word after the first unsuccessful hanging, despite being conscious and realizing what had just happened. Tracy's body was removed from the jail and quietly transported to the Tracy farm, which was three miles outside of town. Fr. Dent officiated over his burial there. Thus ended the second hanging in McKean County history, the first being held in 1850, the year Tracy was born.

The old McKean County Courthouse.

Blackout

Arch Turner's booking photo at the Western Penitentiary.

Two things that do not mix are alcohol and firearms. Statistics show that most homicides and shootings perpetrated by a person under the influence of alcohol were done so accidentally or without clear intentions. A person who has a long history of alcohol abuse could also be subject to something called a blackout. A blackout is when a person has no recollection of what they did or saw or who they interacted with when under the influence. I know one story of a man who drove across Pennsylvania, stopping at fast-food restaurants along the way for two days. He only woke up from this blackout when he returned to his hometown and crashed his car into the local police station. The man had no recollection of ever having left his residence, but the receipts in the backseat of his car proved he had driven over fifteen hundred miles in two days while suffering a blackout. Those who imbibe too much are often told stories the next day of having done something bizarre while under the influence, something they would normally not do when sober. This usually is something they are embarrassed about when shown evidence the following day. The case which follows is an extreme example of an alcoholic blackout.

The Turner and Bennett lumber camp in Norwich Township was situated about halfway between Crosby and Port Allegany, deep in the woods. The camp supplied lumber to the Heinemann Chemical Plant at Crosby. These chemical plants purchased small hardwoods that lumber mills could not use, and through a heating process, they converted this wood into charcoal, methanol (*wood alcohol*), and acetic acid. The tradition at this lumber camp, indeed at all lumber camps, was to celebrate with alcohol on payday, and that is exactly what the men at this camp did on Saturday night, February 9th, 1918, after receiving their pay packets. Two friends, Arch Turner and Edwin (*Eddy*) Ralph, went into Crosby and drank until the morning light, returning to the camp to sleep off the effects on Sunday, which was a day of rest. Ralph woke up around noon and went downstairs to the mess hall and ate a late breakfast with his coworkers. Turner, who had drunk to excess, did not wake up until late in the afternoon and barely ate anything before going back upstairs to his bunk. He had stashed several bottles of whiskey in his locker that he had purchased in Crosby. Turner started drinking again and soon fell asleep from the effects of the whiskey. Turner continued to drink all week, only going downstairs to eat a little meal and once again retiring to his bunk and passing out. He did not go to work this week, and his foreman had told him that if he did not sober up, he would be replaced. This enraged Turner who vowed revenge, but in his intoxicated shape, he fell asleep once again.

On Thursday, February 14th, 1918, Turner was in his daily stupor when Mrs. Sophie Bennett, wife of the owner of the camp, called him to lunch. Turner, who was singing and dancing incoherently, came down the stairs and took a seat next to Ellis Darr, a fellow worker, and Buell Strang, a Crosby woodsman. Eddy Ralph came into the lunch hall and passed the table heading to the kitchen to get himself a drink of water. Turner drunkenly called to him to keep out of the kitchen as he had no damned business going in there. Ralph, knowing that Turner was extremely intoxicated, ignored these remarks and continued into the kitchen. Turner stood up at the table and threatened everyone in the room and began to knock over chairs, saying, "I'll clean out the whole bunch!" Turner then climbed the stairs to the bunk room where he continued to rant and rave about clearing out everyone at the camp. Intermittently he would scream down the stairs to come and get it. Eddy Ralph volunteered to go upstairs and calm Turner down, and he proceeded up the stairs. The men seated in the mess hall watched Turner climb up the stairs, and a moment later, they heard two gunshots and heard a loud thud on the upstairs wooden floor. Silence followed this thud. Buell Strang tiptoed up the stairs and saw the body of Ralph collapsed on the floor in front of Turner, who was bending over the now motionless body of Ralph. Strang went back down the stairs and told everybody that Turner had shot Ralph. Ellis Derr went to seek help from the authorities. Mrs. Bennett then went up the stairs to secure two oil lanterns from the bunkroom as she was worried they would get broken and start a fire. "I'll get you too!" yelled Turner, and Bennett ran back down the stairs and headed out of the cabin to safety. Strang then went back up the stairs and observed Ralph gasping out his last breaths on the floor. He heard Turner tell Ralph, "you make too much noise," and Turner fired again at Ralph, but the shot was wild and went into a wall. Strang made a noise, and Turner saw Strang looking from the top of the stairs. Turner quickly raised his pistol and fired at him, but fortunately the bullet missed. Strang ran back down the stairs and told his coworkers what he had witnessed. Ellis had run to the Heinemann railroad station near the camp, and soon several men followed him back to the lumber camp. One of these men, Nick Carter, accompanied Ellis up the stairs. Seeing Turner sitting on his bunk with the pistol out of his reach, they rushed in and quickly overpowered the intoxicated perpetrator.

The men brought Turner to Crosby on a railway car on Thursday night, and H. H. Gallup and others then transported him to Smethport in Mr. Gallup's automobile.

On Saturday afternoon, a coroner's jury was impaneled in Smethport; H. E. Tull, Michael Hungerford, M. W. Heinieln, F. J.

Nichols, Fred Anderson, and Joseph Meurey composed the jury. The inquest was held at H. H. Sasse's Undertaking Rooms with Acting Coroner Herbert S. Robins presiding. Dr. Burg Chadwick, who performed the autopsy, testified that Edwin Ralph came to his death from a gunshot wound through the brain. After hearing the testimony of Mrs. Sophia Bennett, Buehl Strang, and Ellis Darr, the jury rendered a verdict charging Arch Turner with causing the death of Edwin Ralph.

A hearing was held before Justice R. C. Gleason after the inquest. Justice Gleason ordered Turner to be held without bail to answer to a charge of murder at the term of court convening February 25th. Attorney Guy B. Mayo represented Turner at the hearing, and County Detective Joseph Robertson looked after the Commonwealth's interests at the inquest and the hearing. Turner was taken to the Smethport jail and imprisoned without bail pending his trial later in the month.

The case of Arch Turner charged with the murder of Edwin Ralph on the evening of February 14th was certified to the court of Oyer and Terminer on February 26th, 1918. Upon the court reading the indictment accusing Turner of Ralph's murder, he had previously pled not guilty. Attorney C. W. Catlin, who was appearing for the defendant, offered a motion to withdraw the plea of not guilty and enter a plea of guilty to voluntary manslaughter. District Attorney Wilson acquiesced in the motion, and the court confirmed it. Judge Heck gave Turner an impressive and stern lecture on the consequences of excessive use of alcohol and sentenced Turner to not less than six nor more than seven years in the Western Penitentiary in Pittsburgh. Turner expressed extreme sorrow over the killing of Ralph, a man whom he considered one of his best friends. Turner also stated that he did not remember anything of that week as he had been in an alcoholic blackout and would gladly give his own life if it would bring Ralph back to life.

Funeral services for Edwin "Eddy" Ralph were held from the H. H. Sasse Undertaking Parlors in Smethport on February 21st. Practically nothing was known about the victim, and if he had any relatives, they could not be located. The coroner went through Ralph's meager possessions at the lumber camp but could only guess his age as being fifty-seven. Ralph's body was buried in the Rose Hill Cemetery in Smethport. Arch Turner served his sentence at the Western Penitentiary and was released after six years for good behavior. He returned to the area and settled in Port Allegany, where he had relatives. He eventually established his own business as a carpenter and repented for the rest of his life for the life he took while under the influence of the demon alcohol. Turner died on July 21st, 1943, aged 81 from a heart attack. He was buried in the Portage Valley Cemetery in Wrights.

The Heinemann Chemical Plant in Crosby.

Scandalous

Rose Hill Cemetery in Smethport where Arthur Daily is buried.

One of the most scandalous acts a grown man can commit is to court an underage girl. Despite this being against the law, the raw emotions that this type of relationship elicits from the girl's parents, coupled with the fact that the paramour is much older and married, will bring a reaction that often ends in violence and even death.

One such incident took place in the Rixford-Bradford area back in 1930, and the outcome would prove to be deadly. Gertrude Gemmel of Rixford was a fifteen-year-old Eldred High School student. She was the daughter of Oliver Gemmel *(who had already suffered the loss of a daughter, covered in another story in this book)* who had grown infatuated with twenty-six-year-old Arthur Dailey of Bradford. The much older Dailey enjoyed the attentions of Gertrude, and despite being already married, Dailey believed he could do as he wished and ignored condemnation and scorn from the community and the Gemmel family. Mr. Gemmel had sternly told his daughter that she was not to see Dailey anymore and that he would take matters into his own hands if Dailey continued to pursue her. Gemmel also warned Dailey that he would not accept this relationship and had threatened Dailey on numerous occasions. Dailey and Gertrude continued their secret relationship for some time, and Dailey succeeded in getting Gertrude to disrespect the wishes of her father, and they continued to meet clandestinely. The situation came to a head when Mr. Gemmel confronted Dailey one night in September near his home at Colombia Hill near Rixford. Gemmel admonished Dailey for continuing to see his daughter, and Dailey mercilessly beat the elder Gemmel and told him that the next time he interfered with his relationship with his daughter, he would not be able to walk away. Gertrude saw what her paramour had done to her father but continued to see her lover whenever she could sneak out of her father's watchful eye. The situation came to an explosive ending on Sunday, October 2nd, 1930.

Arthur Kelly, who lived with his mother and stepfather on Forman Street in Bradford, was an uncle to Gertrude by his mother's second marriage. Kelly thought of Gertrude as more of a sister than a niece and was well informed about the tense situation that had developed between Dailey and Oliver Gemmel. Kelly had spent Sunday at the home of his mother. He had brought his aunt Sadie Dibble and her daughter, Ruby, to his mother's house from Eldred, where he had spent Saturday night. The topic of discussion at the Sunday dinner table at his parent's house that day was the relationship of Gertrude Gemmel with the older married Dailey. The discussion became quite heated, and then it was learned that Gertrude had spent the previous night at the Dailey house. Kelly said this could not continue to go on, and he said he was going to the Dailey house and take Gertrude home to her father.

Gertrude's brother Bill, who was at the Sunday dinner, told Kelly where Dailey lived in Tuna and offered to go with him to get her and bring her home. The two left in Kelly's car and drove to the Dailey residence. Bill went to the door and asked for his sister. He was told that she was there but that she did not wish to leave. Bill went back to the car and told Kelly. Kelly, who had secreted a .32 caliber revolver in his right-hand topcoat jacket, then went into the house and found Dailey and Gertrude sitting at the kitchen table. Kelly confronted Gertrude and said her father had forbidden her to visit Dailey's house. Mr. Gemmel had been looking all over for Gertrude. Kelly told Gertrude to get her clothes and that she was going with him to his mother's house and that her father was coming there at 6 to pick her up.

Gertrude replied, "I didn't know he was looking for me, but I am going home the way I intended to, with Art."

Kelly replied, "You're going home with me; there's no use in you causing your dad any more trouble."

Dailey then got out of his chair and grabbed Kelly by the shirt and struck him in the right shoulder with his fist. Kelly told Gertrude she was going with him one way or the other and drew his pistol. Dailey grabbed Kelly's wrist to wrestle the gun out of his grasp, and when he squeezed the wrist, the gun went off. The bullet struck Dailey in the stomach, and he fell backward onto the kitchen floor. Kelly then ran out of the house and got into his car. Dailey appeared at the door with a rifle, and Kelly cowered behind the dash of his vehicle. Dailey shot his rifle at the car and the bullet shattered the windshield and the steering wheel of the Kelly car. A few splinters hit Kelly's face, but he was able to drive away. Kelly returned to Bradford and went to the police headquarters and gave himself up to Officer Harmon.

Dailey was transported to the Bradford hospital, and his condition was reported as very grave due to the injuries he had received. Dailey spent a restless night that Sunday but revived on Monday. On Tuesday, Dailey's pulse quickened, and his resistance began to ebb. He was interviewed by the authorities, and he named Kelly as the shooter. Dailey also said he did not believe he would survive. On Thursday, October 2nd, Dailey succumbed to his injuries and died. His body was moved to the McAllister Funeral Home, where an autopsy was conducted. Coroner H. Clay Heffner conducted an inquest at the funeral home, and the jury found that Arthur Dailey had come to his death by a gunshot fired at the hands of Arthur Kelly.

Arthur Kelly, who had remained in the Bradford jail since he turned himself in on the fateful Sunday afternoon, was formally charged with murder on that Thursday afternoon soon after the coroner's inquest. Kelly was transported to the Smethport jail to await a formal criminal trial.

The body of Arthur Dailey was removed to the home of his brother, L. R. Dailey, at Tuna after the inquest. Funeral services were held on Saturday, October 4th, at his brother's house, and then the service moved to the Davis Community Church under the direction of Rev. Paul Miller. The remains were buried in the Dailey family plot at the Rose Hill Cemetery in Smethport.

The trial of Arthur Kelly commenced in Smethport on Monday, February 23rd, 1931, with the selection of the jury. Kelly was represented by Attorneys Henry Onofrio of Bradford and Claude Shattuck of Smethport. The Commonwealth was represented by Attorney's Wilson and Fitzgibbon of Bradford. Judge Bouton presided.

The prosecution called Dr. S. A. McCutcheon, and he testified that the death of Dailey was caused by a .32 revolver shot to the stomach, which passed through his lower intestines. Death came after a few days due to infection within the body.

Gertrude Gemmel, an eyewitness and the object of the shooting was called next. She reiterated that her uncle, Arthur Kelly, had entered the Dailey residence on that Sunday afternoon. Kelly had told her he was going to take her to her father. She saw Kelly pull a pistol and Dailey grab the wrist which held the pistol. The gun went off and Dailey staggered back and fell onto the floor. Ms. Gemmel said Dailey grabbed a rifle and went after Kelly.

William Gemmel was called next. He told about accompanying his uncle to the Dailey residence and that he saw Kelly put a pistol into his coat as they left their house.

Roscoe Dailey, brother of the deceased, then testified. He said he did not witness the shooting but that he had noticed someone lurking around the residence on the Saturday night prior and that he and his brother had taken a rifle outside to scare the intruder away.

Officer Harmon of the Bradford Police then testified that Kelly came into his office at around 4 o'clock that Sunday afternoon and turned himself in. Harmon repeated the story that Kelly had reported to him, which is substantially the same as was repeated by Gertrude Gemmel. The prosecution then rested.

Oliver Gemmel, the father of Gertrude, was called. He testified about the bad blood between himself and the deceased. Gemmel said Dailey had disrespected all of his wishes and had pummeled him with great ferocity when he confronted Dailey to stop seeing his underage daughter.

Sadie Dibbell was called to testify that Arthur Kelly had spent that Saturday evening at her residence in Eldred and therefore he could not have been the man prowling around the Dailey house that Saturday night.

Arthur Kelly then was called to testify, and he retold the story of how he had been punched by Dailey and had drawn his pistol to intimidate him. He said Dailey then grabbed the hand which held the pistol, and when Dailey squeezed his hand, the weapon fired. Kelly said he had no intentions to kill Dailey and had only brought the weapon with him to intimidate Dailey. Arthur knew Dailey was a dangerous man who had beat up Oliver Gemmel recently and was armed to protect himself.

Judge Bouton sent the case to the jury at 4:30 on Wednesday afternoon, and the jury was out an almost record twenty-two hours before they returned with a verdict of "not guilty" on Thursday afternoon. Arthur Kelly was released from custody to the applause of his family and his friends.

Double Jeopardy

Thelma Davis Smiley shortly before her death.

Wednesday, July 14th, 1948, began like any other day at the Alvin and Thelma Smiley household. Alvin, who had received a physical discharge from the Army due to a back injury, would often be found puttering around their house on Maple Street in Kane. Alvin wore a back brace from this injury and was unable to work steadily. Thelma spent her days taking care of her young children, Patricia, aged two, and Paul, aged one. Thelma has also recently found out she was pregnant with her third child, something she and her husband were reportedly not too thrilled about. At around 2:30 in the afternoon, Alvin suggested that the family take a ride towards Kinzua to break up the monotony of the day. The family car was on old 1936 Plymouth sedan in poor condition. As Mr. Smiley was not steadily employed and only collected a small disability pension from the military, the family could not afford a more modern car. With all four occupying the front seat of the sedan, the family headed out towards Kinzua Road. About a mile and a half outside of Kane, Mrs. Smiley asked her husband to pull over as her son was fussing and would need to be fed. Smiley pulled the sedan onto the side of the road, and Mrs. Smiley climbed into the back seat and began to bottle feed her baby. Mr. Smiley remained in the front seat with his two-year-old daughter. Smiley started out again, and when in second gear and entering the roadway, he heard the sound of a shot nearby and heard his wife cry, "Al!" Smiley stopped his car and looked in the rear-view mirror and saw his wife slump forward over the baby, with blood pouring out of a wound over her eye. Smiley jumped out of the driver's seat and picked up Mrs. Smiley, so she did not smother the baby and realized that the noise he had heard was from a bullet entering the vehicle. Smiley could see that his wife was bleeding badly from the wound, and after placing the baby away from the mortally wounded mother, he immediately turned the car around and headed towards Kane and the hospital. About one and a half miles from Kane, Smiley pulled his car over by a set of cabins and asked two youths walking there to help him get his wife to the hospital. He told the boys that she had been hit by a "stray" bullet. The boys climbed in with Mr. Smiley and accompanied him to the hospital.

Laura Johnson, RN, had just arrived at the Kane Area Hospital for her shift on Wednesday, July 14th, 1948, when she was immediately summoned to the emergency room. As Laura made her way to the emergency room, she was confronted by a hysterical man carrying a young woman, bleeding profusely from an apparent head wound.

Johnson led the man to the nearest examination table and began to attend to the woman. Johnson checked the unconscious woman's vital signs and still found a pulse. She summoned the physician on call, Dr. L. W. Dana, to the emergency room. Dr. Dana was at his private residence on this weekday afternoon, and it took him fifteen minutes to reach the hospital. Dr. Dana found a young woman with no signs of life, and after a cursory examination, he noted a bullet hole in her head, just above her right eye. The authorities had already arrived and were busy questioning the deceased's husband, the man who had brought this woman to the hospital. The deceased was identified as Thelma Davis Smiley, nineteen years of age and the mother of two young children. Mrs. Smiley was also pregnant when she met her demise. Kane's normally quiet town was about to find out that one of its precious souls had died most suspiciously.

Kane Police Chief Bernard Rose soon arrived at the hospital shortly followed by State Trooper Robert Hauth. Rose and Hauth interviewed Smiley, and he provided the story about the "stray" bullet and described the shooting scene as being around two and a half miles from Kane on the Kinzua Road. McKean County Detective Merle Dickinson and County Coroner Elmer Beatty then arrived. Rose and Hauth headed out toward the shooting scene to put a ring around the area to catch the "unknown" gunner who had fired the fatal shot. All available policemen joined the two lawmen in the area, but no sign of a gunman was found. Smiley was transported to the "scene" of the shooting by Dickinson and Beatty. When questioned further about the shot, Smiley said it sounded like a .22 caliber, but it could have been an air rifle or pistol. He said it sounded like it came from a distance of about one hundred yards.

Smiley calmly told his story and only added that he wished it had been himself and what would happen to the babies? A complete check of the area was conducted, but no one was found with a weapon, much less one that had recently fired one. The location that Smiley had identified was one hundred and fifty yards north of the Rudolph

Anderson Camp and almost directly opposite a camp owned by Cameron Weaver. Police stopped all vehicles entering and leaving the area to question the occupants, but all denied hearing a shot or knowing of anyone in the area that afternoon. Smiley showed where his car was parked and indicated the point from which the bullet came from. The police thoroughly searched the site where the suspected shooter would have had to have been standing to make a shot, such as that described by Smiley. Smiley was then transported back to the hospital, where photos were taken of the interior of his car. Smiley left the hospital to return to his Maple Street home to change his blood-spattered clothing, and then went to a *Kane Republican* reporters' home with photos of his wife, which he had promised earlier. He then went to the State Police Substation with his vehicle.

Suspicion was mounting in the onsite investigation when experts determined that it would have been an impossibility for a bullet to have traveled into the back seat of the sedan from where Smiley had indicated the shot came from. From the direction that Smiley identified, there was an almost vertical drop of twenty feet. For a bullet to travel at an upward angle from that depth and still pierce the front of the sedan and strike Mrs. Smiley in the backseat of the sedan was a physical impossibility. The searchers at the scene found three empty .22 caliber cartridges and two loaded .22 bullets within two hundred feet of where Smiley had indicated his sedan was parked.

The state troopers then conducted a thorough inspection of the Smiley sedan. They found one bullet hole with probable powder burns in the passenger door's fabric covering. A slug, smashed by partial contact with the window's metal operation mechanism, was found lying on the passenger side floor. Two other holes were noted in the machine's roof, and both holes appeared to be new and caused by bullets. Further examination of these holes indicated that they had been fired from within the vehicle as stuffing had been pushed through the openings. The holes were spaced about six inches apart and directly over the passenger seat.

Based on these and the findings out in the field, Smiley was transported to the Kane Borough jail to be held pending charges which were expected to be filed. Smiley continued to stick to his story but was beginning to hint that he had not told what had really happened.

The Kane Police removed Smiley to the McKean County jail during the night. The investigation continued throughout the night. In the morning, the investigators requested that Smiley be brought back to Kane for further interrogation, as the authorities had determined several severe discrepancies in Smiley's story.

Alvin Smiley was once again interviewed at the police headquarters on Thursday, July 15th, in Kane. At first, he continued to stick by his story of the stray bullet. When confronted by the evidence that his account of a stray shot was impossible from the location he had described, Smiley changed his story. He admitted that he owned a .22 rifle and that he had taken this along on his trip to shoot groundhogs. Smiley then told officials that he was traveling along the highway towards Kinzua when he stopped the car after seeing a woodchuck run down an embankment. Smiley exited the vehicle but was not quick enough to get a shot at the varmint. He said he returned to the car and found that his wife had slid over to the driver's side of the vehicle and wanted to drive. Smiley said he told his wife that the car was in no condition for her to drive, as it had many mechanical problems. Thelma then moved back to the passenger side of the vehicle.

The baby then began "fussing," and Mrs. Smiley exited the front seat and entered the rear seat to feed the baby. The other child remained in the front seat with Smiley. Smiley then said he placed the rifle on the passenger side's floorboard with the barrel pointing toward the top of the car. He said he started onto the highway when the gun discharged, and he heard his wife cry out. Smiley stopped the auto and then noticed his wife slumped over the baby in the backseat. Smiley said he pulled the baby from underneath his wife and placed the child on the seat. He then started to drive towards Kane, and en route, he stopped and got out of his car and took the gun and threw it into the woods. Smiley also discarded a pocketful of shells at the same place. Smiley said he told the first version of the events about the "stray" bullet because he was in a panic and that he threw the gun and bullets away because he "never wanted to see them again."

Smiley was then transported back to the Kinzua Road to help authorities find the murder weapon. He pointed out an area with a high, bare bank as the missing gun's location. Searchers began canvassing that area for the weapon, and Smiley was transported back to the State Police barracks for further questioning. The searchers were unsuccessful in finding the rifle and called upon the local National Guard barracks for help searching for the weapon with their mine detectors. Smiley was once again questioned on the weapon's location and transported back to the highway a second time. This time he picked out an almost identical area as the first location and stated he was mistaken on the first location. Searchers began to walk throughout this second location and successfully found the weapon just as the Kane National Guard soldiers arrived with their mine detecting equipment. The rifle had been found tossed into the high ferns alongside the road, about twenty feet from the highway. The gun was found to have sixteen loaded shells in the magazine and one empty cartridge in the chamber. The weapon was also missing the trigger guard.

Coroner Elmer Beaty called an inquest on Thursday afternoon in the offices of Justice of the Peace Emile Stenger. The jury was composed of J. M. Harre, foreman, Lloyd P. Thompson, Mike Fragale, Thomas Woodward, Paul Bloomquist, and O G. Brown.

The first witness called was Dr. Robert B. Donaldson, who conducted the post-mortem at the Cummings Funeral Home in Kane on Wednesday evening. Dr. Donaldson testified on the cause of death being "a bullet which entered at the right eye and traveled an upward course to the base of the brain." The doctor stated that the hemorrhage and severe brain damage had been caused by fragments of the bullet. He then displayed an x-ray negative to show the location of the fragments and the bullet. Dr. Donaldson turned the bullet over to McKean County Detective Merle Dickinson after his testimony finished.

The second witness called was State Police Trooper Robert Hauth. Hauth told of the Kane Community Hospital's telephone call reporting the shooting and the investigation that followed. He reiterated the story, which Smiley initially told regarding the stray bullet. Hauth said Smiley changed his story when confronted with the impossibility of a shot being fired from the direction that Smiley had identified and striking his vehicle in the way he had reported. Hauth then testified that when he confronted Smiley on this discrepancy, Smiley then told the version that the shot was fired inside of the vehicle by "accident." Hauth told the jury that Smiley could not explain why he gave the false story other than he was in a panic and wanted to get rid of the gun and shells. Hauth then testified about finding bullets and spent shells at the crime scene. He said that these bullets were obviously dropped by another person as they did not match the ammo that was later found in the rifle magazine.

Police Chief Bernard Rose testified on receiving the hospital's call and how he set up a roadblock in the area of the shooting to check people coming out of the area. Rose then told about statements Smiley had originally made about the stray shot and subsequent statements that were not before the jury.

Jim Hillman, a member of the search party that hunted Wednesday night and Thursday morning for the gun, testified how he found the rifle. Hillman described the gun's position when found and of how the magazine was loaded with live rounds with one empty shell in the chamber. Hillman also stated that the weapon did not have a trigger guard.

McKean County Detective Merle Dickinson then testified on various phases of the investigation. Dickinson spoke at length about the shooting scene and how it was determined to have been an impossibility for the fatal shot being fired from the direction that Smiley initially indicated. Dickinson also spoke about the "three" bullet holes found in the Smiley vehicle. The detective testified as to how all were determined to have been made from the inside, and none had been found to have been made from the outside. Dickinson told of how the searchers had found the weapon after searching two locations and that the gun had sixteen live rounds loaded in the magazine and one spent cartridge in the chamber. He also clarified that the shells found earlier by the scene of the shooting did not match the shells found in the weapon and were probably discarded at an earlier date by another person.

The testimony was then completed, and the jury retired to make their verdict. The jury returned with the judgment that "Mrs. Thelma Davis Smiley met her death by a bullet from a .22 rifle owned by her husband Alvin Smiley, which was in the automobile at the time of her death."

Following the inquest, Dickinson stated that "charges would be preferred in this case," but indicated that additional details needed clearing before definitive action would be taken. Dickinson said he would consult with the district attorney and would have further information available the following day.

Thelma Davis Smiley was born in Kane on May 8th, 1929, to John and Goldie Boyd Davis. She was nineteen years old at the time of her death and the mother of a daughter, Patricia, aged two, and a one-year-old son, Paul. She was also pregnant with her third child. She was married to Alvin Aquilla Smiley and resided at 118 Maple Street in Kane. The wake and funeral services for Thelma were held at her parents' home, which was located at 520 Biddle Street. Over one thousand people visited the house on Friday night, July 16th, and police were required to handle traffic on the street as a result of so many mourners. Funeral rites were held on Saturday afternoon from the residence. Alvin Smiley was transported from his jail cell to attend. The parents of Thelma had asked the district attorney to allow Alvin to attend to pay his final respects. Smiley reportedly broke down at the sight of his dead wife and was seen to mouth condolences to her parents. He was returned to the McKean County jail after the services ended. Reverend Sherman H. Epler, pastor of the First Methodist Church, conducted the services. Pallbearers were Cecil Zentz, Ernest Evans, Philipp John, Eugene Keener, and Lloyd Chamberlain. Burial took place in the Davis family plot in the Forest Lawn Cemetery.

Smiley remained in the McKean County jail while Detective Dickinson and Trooper Hauth continued to investigate the evidence they had discovered in the case. The most intriguing evidence was the unexplained bullet holes in the Smiley vehicle. Smiley had stated he only accidentally fired one shot, which struck his wife in the forehead. This bullet was found during the autopsy of Mrs. Smiley. What Smiley did not explain was how another bullet had been fired inside the vehicle, which resulted in damage to the passenger side window. This bullet was found on the passenger-side floorboard. Also unexplained were the two holes in the vehicle's roof, which appeared to have been fired from inside the automobile. Smiley did not explain these three additional bullet holes and claimed they were not present after his wife was fatally shot. The police were also concentrating on the rifle. The trigger guard appeared to have been purposely removed and investigators wondered why this would have been done. The rifle was also noted to have been a bolt action, and this would require someone to eject a fired bullet before the rifle could fire again. Canvassing of the area of the shooting continued, but no one was located who saw the Smiley family or heard a shot during the time the shooting took place. A lie detector test was discussed as possibly being used but this was put off for the time being. As Judge Charles G. Hubbard was on vacation at the time of the shooting, the district attorney had to wait for his return to file charges and have Judge Hubbard appoint defense counsel for Smiley.

Judge Hubbard returned from his vacation, and one of the first tasks he performed was appointing Attorneys Ralph DeCamp of Kane and Robert Apple of Smethport as counsel to Smiley. District Attorney Claude Shattuck represented the Commonwealth and charged Smiley with murder in the death of his wife.

A formal arraignment on the charge of first-degree murder was held at the office of Justice of the Peace Stenger in Kane on Friday, July 23rd, 1948. County Detective Merle Dickinson was the charging officer. The hearing opened with Detective Dickinson being sworn in by Justice Stenger, and Dickinson read out the allegations and charges, which were intentional "willful murder." Smiley pled "not guilty" to these charges.

Trooper Robert Hauth was the first witness called. Hauth testified about the initial call he received from the Kane Community Hospital and of the subsequent investigation.

Coroner Elmer Beatty, Dr. Robert Donaldson, Police Chief Bernard Rose, State Police Trooper Robert Bamat, James Hillman, William Gustafson, Robert Magnuson, and Detective Dickinson, then testified in order of their participation in the investigation. All told of their connections with the case and the extensive investigation which had been underway since the shooting had occurred at around 2:30 p. m. on July 14th.

William Gustafson and Robert Magnuson identified themselves as the two youths who were picked up on the Kinzua Road by Smiley on his way to the hospital. Both stated that Smiley asked them to hold onto the children in the car and that his wife had been shot by a stray bullet.

James Hillman testified about his involvement in the search for the gun and of its eventual finding. Hillman identified the weapon as a .22 caliber Marlin bolt action rifle.

Detective Dickinson then testified about his involvement in the investigation and brought out that three bullet holes were found in the death vehicle, and neither of Smiley's two versions of events could explain their presence.

Defense Attorney DeCamp then presented Smiley's third version of the shooting, which had never been heard before. Smiley claimed that the bullet hole in the passenger side door was because the gun had accidentally discharged twice. The first time the bullet struck his wife. Smiley claimed to have reached over and threw the bolt after the first shot and had ejected the empty cartridge, and a new shell was automatically placed in the chamber by this action. Smiley said that the butt of the gun was resting on the floorboards and the stock on the seat at this time. As Smiley turned the car to bring his wife to the hospital, the gun fell and struck the door, discharging the second time. In this third version of events, Smiley held that he had no knowledge of the other two holes in the roof of the car.

All of the police officers present were then questioned by both District Attorney Shattuck and Defense Attorney DeCamp as to whether or not the additional two holes in the roof of the car were, in fact, bullet holes. None of the officers could say with one hundred percent accuracy that the holes in the vehicle's ceiling had come from bullets.

A move was then made by Defense Attorney DeCamp to bring in the results of a lie detector test that had been performed on Smiley. Shattuck blocked this move because the test was not brought out as evidence. DeCamp entered an exception to the objection, but Shattuck's objection was sustained by Stenger.

Smiley was observed to have been listening closely during the arraignment and showed no emotion except when the rifle with the missing trigger guard was examined for identification purposes. Smiley turned his head when the gun was held up for the court to view.

After all the evidence was presented, Justice Stenger ordered Smiley to be held without bail on the murder charges connected with the death of his wife. He would face a grand jury on the charges at the October term of court. Smiley was returned to the McKean County jail immediately after the arraignment.

Smiley's attorneys filed a writ of habeas corpus on September 18th with Judge Hubbard. They asked for Smiley's release on bail while he awaited trial. Judge Hubbard called a hearing on October 1st in Smethport. After listening to the evidence presented by the Commonwealth and the arguments provided by the defense, Judge Hubbard ruled that the Commonwealth's evidence was not sufficient in substantiating the first-degree murder charge. He ruled, "The court was not convinced that it would be justified under the evidence produced at the hearing in refusing to admit the petitioner to bail. Such refusal in the opinion of the court would be a denial of his constitutional rights." Smiley was released on $5,000 cash bail and returned to his home to await further proceedings. Evidence which the defense did present at this hearing was the fact that Smiley had passed a lie detector test back in July during the initial investigation. Smiley's attorneys also filed a request for a continuance in the case to permit Smiley to receive medical attention and to give additional time to prepare the case as a result of delays in securing his army records. It was noted that Smiley suffered a disabling back injury while in basic training with the U. S. Army and wore a back brace as a result. Judge Hubbard took this into consideration.

The grand jury of McKean County met on Tuesday, October 5th, 1948, in Smethport and indicted Alvin Smiley on a murder charge in the death of his wife. Judge Charles G. Hubbard also refused a continuance in a hearing on motions by his defense counsel. When reached later at his home in Kane, Smiley stated that he was glad that the continuance was denied and hoped "to get it all over with" as soon as possible. Smiley continued to maintain that the shooting was accidental, and that shock and fear had caused him to give his early versions of a stray bullet.

In the months between his indictment and the future trial, Smiley kept himself busy by working odd jobs in the Kane area. Rumors were rampant that Smiley had a "secret" lover, and this was one of the reasons why he murdered his wife. Other's speculated that Smiley did not want another child, and this was the reason for the shooting. The Smiley family stood by their son and supported his version of events to whoever would listen. The Kane community wanted justice, and the wait for the trial seemed endless. On December 10th, 1948, a special term of the McKean County Court set the trial date for Alvin Smiley for January 17th. Smiley would then face a jury trial, which could very well end his life if he was convicted of first-degree murder.

Jury selection for the trial of the Commonwealth versus Alvin Smiley commenced on Monday, January 17th, in the McKean County Courthouse in Smethport. Jury selection took over three days, with the chief objection to prospective jurors being their views of voting for capital punishment based on circumstantial evidence. The selection process called over one hundred and ninety prospective jurors, such a large number being unheard of. All residents of Kane and the surrounding areas were excluded because of pre-trial publicity. The jurors selected were Wright Scroxton, Mrs. Agnes Harvender, Sangster Hawley, Earl K Dana, James McKittrick, all from Bradford; Lynn Abby, Allee Diegel, Charles McGivern, Elmer Quirk of Smethport; Mrs. Dorothy Cummings and Glen Turner of Eldred and Harry Boudon Jr. of Port Allegany. The jurors were all sequestered into a local hotel for the duration of the trial, forbidden from having any contact with family or the public. Smiley, however, was still out on bail and returned to his home each night after the proceedings.

The trial began on Thursday afternoon, January 20th. The first action at court was a fierce objection by Defense Counsel Robert Apple to the appointment of Special Assistant District Attorney Joseph P. Wilson to assist District Attorney Claude Shattuck. Shattuck had not even had a chance to present his opening address to the jury when Apple objected on the grounds that a special prosecutor in the case was in violation of statutes. Judge Hubbard ruled that he could think of no murder case in which an assistant prosecutor was not appointed. Hubbard pointed out to Apple that the reason he appointed two defense counsels for Smiley was partly in case Apple should become ill during the trial. Judge Hubbard also ruled that any objection for an assistant prosecutor should have been made before trial and that Wilson was appointed in October. The appointment of Wilson remained, and Apple was overruled.

District Attorney Shattuck then made the opening address. He sketched the Smiley case from the initial call received from the Kane Hospital at 3:20 p. m. on July 14th, 1948, through to the time the defendant was ordered held for murder at his arraignment in Kane. The address took twenty minutes.

Shattuck called Trooper Robert Hauth as his first witness. Hauth testified that he received the call from the Kane Hospital at 3:20 p. m. on July 14th and arrived at the hospital within a few minutes. He was advised by Mrs. Marjorie Haese, acting superintendent of the hospital, that Mrs. Thelma Smiley had died in the emergency room. Hauth stated that Mr. Smiley and Mrs. John Davis, mother of Mrs. Smiley, were at the hospital.

Coroner Elmer C. Beatty was next called to the stand. He testified to receiving the call from the hospital concerning a fatality, and upon arriving at the hospital, he asked the family to which funeral home did they desire for the body to be taken. He ordered the body taken to the Cummings Funeral Home and arranged a post-mortem to be conducted by Dr. Robert Donaldson, a staff physician at the Kane Hospital. The post-mortem took place at 7 p. m. on July 14th.

Dr. Donaldson was then called to the stand. He read his autopsy report and described the path of the bullet entering at the corner of the right eye, passing through the eye in an upward and outward direction.

He stated that when he was examining the bullet hole in the brain, a piece of bullet dropped to the table. This piece of the bullet was entered into evidence. The doctor also said fragments remained in the brain of Mrs. Smiley. He reported no other signs of violence on the body and that her body was normal and healthy. He started to report on the pregnancy of Mrs. Smiley when Defense Attorney Apple vigorously opposed the testimony on the grounds that it was irrelevant and immaterial. District Attorney Wilson opposed this motion on the grounds that the prosecution desired the pregnancy report for its purpose of a motive. The objection was overruled, and the doctor reported that Mrs. Smiley was between two and three months pregnant at the time of her death.

Trooper Hauth then returned to the stand for cross-examination by Apple. After repeating his previous testimony regarding the initial call he received, Hauth then related the "stray bullet" story, discovery of the bullet hole and the bullet in the car, the change in Smiley's story, and of the later alterations to the story in which Smiley told of the two accidental discharges of the gun in the car and how Smiley threw the weapon away on his way back to Kane.

County Detective Merle Dickinson next took the stand. He told of being called to Kane at around 4 p. m. on July 14th. He reiterated Smiley's first statement regarding the stray bullet and then how Smiley's statement changed when presented with the bullet hole evidence, which did not reconcile with the stray bullet story. The detective then introduced the evidence of a fourth bullet hole in the car for the first time. This evidence was a bombshell. The authorities had previously stated that there were three probable bullet holes shot from inside the auto; however, Smiley had explained one of the holes as having been caused when he fired a second shot accidentally after the first fatal shot had struck his wife. Detective Dickinson went on to explain that two holes found in the roof of the car were not bullet holes, despite supposedly having not been in the auto roof on that fateful day, according to Smiley. Dickinson said while the two holes in the roof were not bullet holes and were a mystery, another hole found in the back portion of the front seat was most certainly a bullet hole, which could not be accounted for by any of Smiley's version of events. Dickinson testified that this could not have been made by the shot which killed Mrs. Smiley due to the angle it was fired. Dickinson said this would mean Smiley would have had to eject the spent shells twice for all three shots to have fired "accidentally." He also testified that after many tests performed on the alleged death weapon, his staff had been unable to get the weapon to accidentally fire, no matter how many times they knocked it over exactly how Smiley described. Dickinson was rigorously cross-examined by Apple regarding statements that the bullet holes could not have been caused by the weapon falling as Smiley described. Apple did get an admission from Dickinson that if Mrs. Smiley had been sitting on the very edge of the back seat and leaning forward nursing the baby, she could have been hit by the bullet hole discovered in the front seat portion. Dickinson then introduced a statement that Smiley had given and signed in which Smiley admitted changing his story from the original stray bullet story and later giving the third version after presented with further evidence.

James Hillman briefly testified next concerning finding the .22 rifle, which had allegedly caused the death of Mrs. Smiley. The next witnesses were William Gustafson and Robert Magnuson, Kane High School students whom Smiley picked up on the way to the hospital. Both testified that Smiley told them that his wife had been hit by a stray bullet.

Mrs. Pearl Kraft, Kane store operator, was next called, and she reported a conversation with Smiley on the morning of the day his wife was shot. Kraft said that when Smiley was in her store, he said, "Sometimes, I wish I had never married." She said she asked him, "What do you mean?" He replied, "there are so many nice girls running around." She queried further, "you mean the ones who just left the store?" "No," he replied, "like the one that just passed the store!"

Trooper Robert Bamat and Sergeant Elmer J. Botteflier, a chemist for the state police laboratory, then testified to collecting and testing patches from the four holes found in the Smiley vehicle. The hole found in the passenger side door and the rear of the front seat both tested positive for powder burn marks and were positively identified as having come from recent bullets. The two holes in the roof were also tested but lacked the existence of powder burns and could not be determined to have come from a bullet.

Kane Police Chief Bernard Rose then testified as to his involvement with the case and interactions with Smiley. Rose said that when he was still following the stray bullet story, he asked Smiley if he owned a gun. He said Smiley told him he had one previously but had sold it to a man in Clarion. Rose also testified that when he was checking the line of fire on the door of the Smiley automobile, he noted a .22 shell on the floor of the passenger side. He then checked the car and found a part of the bullet lodged in the passenger door well and three other holes in the vehicle.

Mr. and Mrs. John Davis, parents of Mrs. Smiley, both testified that the couple, Mr. and Mrs. Smiley, had said they did not want any more children. Several more individuals testified to their involvement at the hospital when Mrs. Smiley was brought into the emergency room. The prosecution then rested.

Immediately after the prosecution rested, defense counsel Robert Apple entered a demurrer asking the court to release Smiley on the grounds that the state had failed to produce evidence for a murder charge. Mr. Apple argued that the Commonwealth had built up what amounted to an involuntary manslaughter case, citing that there was no eye witness, no confession of guilt, no motive, and all evidence was purely circumstantial with nothing to support a murder conviction. Apple said, "if pregnancy is any cause for murder, the human race is doomed for extinction." He added that the lies or versions told by the defendant are not sufficient proof of guilt.

Attorney Wilson argued for the Commonwealth. "We have a prima facie case in which the jury is entitled to hear the evidence. Wilson cited the removal of the trigger guard of the rifle, taking a fully loaded rifle into the car, the safety of the rifle left off for both admitted accidental discharges, and the "defendant did not lie only once, but lied for five consecutive days." Wilson also discussed the pregnancy motive.

Judge Hubbard, after reviewing both the defense and prosecution arguments, denied the motion.

Attorney DeCamp then began the defense by delivering a half-hour address to the jury in which he reviewed Smiley's background and the events of his life up to the shooting. He pointed out that Smiley was mentally deficient and had a hard time complying with school requirements. That Smiley was unable to hold a job and that he was unqualified for Army service. DeCamp also described the back-injury Smiley had received in the Army, which had caused Smiley much pain and required regular treatment from the Veteran's Administration. DeCamp said Smiley had never been in trouble before this date.

Mrs. S. A. Smiley, mother of the defendant, was the first defense witness called. She reiterated the previous statements that DeCamp had said and stated that while her son was mentally deficient, he had always been a law-abiding citizen. Smiley's father was next, and he noted that the car Smiley was driving on the day of the shooting was in lousy shape and difficult to maneuver. He gave this evidence to show that the mile Smiley had driven after the shooting to turn around was necessary due to the extreme difficulty maneuvering the auto.

Giennes H. Rickart, Superintendent of the Kane Schools, verified that Smiley had failed to achieve school grades with the other members of his class. Rickart testified that Smiley took two years for each grade and left school at eighteen while enrolled in the eighth grade.

The main witness for the defense, Alvin Smiley himself, was then called to the stand after a few minor witnesses. Smiley's voice was described as so low that his attorneys had to ask him to speak up. Smiley testified about his upbringing, school, employment, and Army service. Smiley then told of the fateful day, July 14th, 1948. He told of hastily assembling the gun at his home as his wife and children prepared for a ride. He grabbed a handful of shells and placed them in his pocket. All four of them were in the front seat. Smiley loaded the gun only a few feet outside the borough and put the gun at his left, next to the door, and started down the highway watching for woodchucks.

Smiley said two miles from Kane, he saw a woodchuck scamper across the road and stopped to try to get a shot. He said he couldn't get a shot and walked back to the car. At this time, his wife entered the back seat of the car to feed the baby. Smiley placed the loaded rifle with the butt resting on the floorboard and the barrel pointing towards the backseat of the auto. Smiley said he had "just started to drive onto the road when the gun discharged...I automatically reached down and ejected the empty shell and at the same time heard my wife cry out "Al." I turned and saw her slumped over to the left, partially covering the baby who was crying. I stopped the car, got out, and took the baby into the front seat. I then started down the road to turn around, and as I swung the car around, the rifle fell, and as the barrel struck the door, it was discharged again." With the car in motion, he indicated he picked up the gun, reached over and laid the gun on the rear floor, and headed to the hospital. He said he stopped along the way to throw away the rifle and shells. Smiley said he picked up the two high school boys to help hold his children, so they did not fall off of the front seat and hurt themselves. Smiley reiterated his involvement in the investigation and how, when shown there was a second and possibly more bullet holes in the car, that he did not remember a second shot going off in the car. He said it was only later that he recalled the gun went off the second time.

Decamp asked Smiley point-blank: "Did you intend to kill your wife?"

"No!" Smiley replied.

"Did you ever think of harming your wife?"

"No," "I never noticed the guard was off; my hand was on the pistol grip of the rifle."

"Did you re-cock the rifle after it had discharged?"

"I must have from a force of habit."

Asked about the safety latch on the rifle, Smiley said he did not use it because it had gone off once before.

Closely questioned on the time required to reach the hospital, Smiley was asked if he had examined his wife in the car.

"No, I was afraid if I monkeyed around, it might make it worse," he replied.

District Attorney Claude Shattuck then began the cross-examination. He attacked the stray bullet story and worked the angle that this was premeditated murder.

"When you started on your trip, you had the gun at your left?"

"Yes."

"Did you know the safe was off?"

"Yes"

"Did you deny knowing the trigger guard was off?"

"Yes."

"Your memory of the stray bullet was good. Why did you lie if it was an accident?"

" I was afraid no one would believe me."

"Didn't you set this gun and lure your wife into range to pull the trigger?"

"No!"

Smiley then was left off of the stand, and the defense rested.

Defense Attorney Apple then began the closing summation for the defense. He stressed that the presumption of innocence prevailed in this case. That Smiley had a lack of motive and no record of any kind of trouble. He told the jury, "You can't guess the defendant into a charge of murder!" Apple referred to the defendant as a "scared kid" with an eighth-grade brain. The defense then rested.

Assistant District Attorney Wilson began the prosecution's closing arguments by demonstrating the way the state claimed Mrs. Smiley met death "that she was lured into a position, and Smiley pulled the trigger." He cited the pregnancy motive, the testimony of Mrs. Pearl Kraft, the safety of the gun being off and the trigger guard missing. This he declared "follows the pattern of a planned accident." The prosecution then rested.

Judge Hubbard then began his charge to the jury, explaining the indictment that Smiley "feloniously, willfully and with malice aforethought killed and murdered his wife." He cited various verdicts possible, either murder in the first-degree with either death or life imprisonment, murder in the second-degree, with the court fixing punishment or acquittal. The judge commented on the "many facts in the case which were not disputed." He cited two points for the prosecution and affirmed one. He listed thirty-one points for the defense, affirming half.

The jury left the courtroom to render a decision. The bells to the courthouse began ringing after fifty minutes, signaling a verdict, and the jury returned to the courtroom. Wright Scroxton, the foreman, handed the verdict to the prothonotary, Joseph Carvolth. Carvolth passed the verdict to Judge Hubbard, who returned it to Carvolth for reading. Mr. Carvolth read, "We the jury find Alvin A. Smiley not guilty."

Smiley, his eyes filled with tears, turned to his parents, who were only a few feet away. Smiley and his parents moved over to the jury box to express their gratitude. Outrage was expressed by many both in and outside of the courthouse.

Alvin Smiley left the courthouse with his parents and returned to his residence in Kane, a free man. The overflow crowd at the courthouse was in disbelief that this man, who had admitted negligence in handling the rifle that killed his wife, was now free. District Attorney Shattuck and Attorney Wilson, however, were busy preparing another round of charges. They surmised that although Smiley was acquitted of the charge of murder, they could still charge Smiley with involuntary manslaughter, a misdemeanor, and thereby not commit the offense of "double-jeopardy."

Smiley had returned to Kane and resumed his recently acquired job at the Johnson Brother's Meat Market. On Friday afternoon, January 28th, Detective Merle Dickinson, accompanied by State Trooper Bamat, served Smiley with an arrest warrant at his job, and Smiley was taken in front of Justice Stenger. Smiley, through his attorney, Ralph DeCamp, waived his hearing and was released on $500 bail. Smiley also faced a charge for violation of the state game laws. The maximum sentence Smiley could receive for the involuntary manslaughter charge was three years, with a five-year hunting license suspension on the game charge. Smiley was advised that his new case would be scheduled for the next term of court, which was to begin on February 28th.

The Kane townsfolk and indeed many in McKean County felt that Smiley had gotten away with murder, plain and simple. Rumors had been circulating since the shooting that Smiley had another girl and that this was the reason for the shooting. The rumors reached a head in February of 1949 when even the prosecution had to make an investigation of these rumors, and Smiley and his family also had to release a statement to the press that there was "nothing to it." No paramour of Smiley was ever credibly found.

As February 28th arrived, the word that Smiley would plead guilty to the new charges reached the community. Smiley's attorneys confirmed this rumor, and Smiley issued a statement that said, "I think it is best for my family and myself, and to satisfy the public" in announcing his pending guilty plea.

Alvin Smiley entered the McKean County Courthouse on March 3rd, accompanied by his father, John Smiley, to plead guilty to involuntary manslaughter in the death of his wife. District Attorney Shattuck made a brief statement that he resented recent reports in the local papers presenting this second arrest as a persecution and felt that Smiley needed to be held accountable for causing the death of his wife. Defense Attorney DeCamp made a statement that while his client was indeed guilty of causing the accidental death of his wife, that he had already spent three months in jail and had also suffered the loss of his wife, and therefore had paid for his "accidental" crime. Judge Hubbard admonished Smiley for the reckless behavior concerning the loaded weapon and the careless handling of the rifle, which caused the death of Mrs. Smiley. "I have had many cases in my life," he stated, "but never anything to touch this case, the rashness, the reckless disregard for life. There is no disputing the facts; his wife and children were in danger every minute they were in the jostling car!" Smiley stated he had no comment when asked by the Judge if he had anything to say.

Judge Hubbard then sentenced Smiley to a two-year term in the Allegheny County Workhouse, to commence as soon as arrangements could be made. He also lost his hunting privileges for five years. Smiley was transported to the Smethport jail and, in due order, reported to the workhouse in Pittsburgh. Smiley served his two-year sentence and returned to Kane after his parole. He eventually remarried to a Miss Virginia Simmons on December 24th, 1952, and moved to Salamanca, New York. Alvin Smiley died on January 21st, 2004, in Salamanca at the age of 81. He is buried in the Riverside Cemetery in Pittsfield, Warren County, next to his second wife. Whether the shooting was a careless accident or something else was taken to the grave by Alvin Smiley. A sorrowful story indeed.

Thelma's grave in Forest Lawn Cemetery in Kane

You Belong to Me

Vernon Thoren

Murder-suicides are one of the saddest situations where an innocent person's life is at the mercy of a deranged individual. These types of murders often occur during the breakup of a romantic relationship. The murderer cannot accept rejection and somehow imagines that ending both of the couple's lives will remedy the situation. The families of the victims are left to wonder what they could have done to stop such madness, and how their loved one had reached the decision to become a murderer. Sadly, there often are no clues that parents or friends could have noticed that would have prevented these acts of desperate emotions. One such incident shattered the innocence of Port Allegany during the Second World War. This act would never be forgotten for the sadness and emptiness which followed the loss of two promising young adults.

On a bright and sunny day, June 6, 1943, two young boys walked to the community park in Port Allegany to see if the community swimming pool had finally been filled and ready for swimmers. The youths, Donald Quint, sixteen, and Jerry Quint, twelve, were brothers and the sons of Mr. and Mrs. Albert Quint. While the two boys were at the pool, they noticed a sports coupe parked in the rear of the bathhouse. They walked up to the car and were horrified to see the body of a man slumped over the wheel, and the body of a woman laying across his lap. The boys ran to their house and told their parents what they had found. Mr. Quint called Port Allegany Chief of Police Albert Clauser, who, accompanied by several officers, went to the park to investigate. After a quick determination that they had two dead people, Clauser contacted Coroner Clark and County Detective Merle Dickinson.

County Coroner Clark, assisted by Detective Dickinson, searched the possessions of the deceased and found their identifications. They identified the young woman as Miss Joan Herger, twenty-two, the socially prominent daughter of Mr. and Mrs. Howard C. Herger of Port Allegany. The man was Vernon Thoren, twenty-one, son of Mr. and Mrs. Harold A. Thoren, of Two Mile, just outside of the Borough of Port Allegany.

The bodies were transported to the Grabe Funeral Home to conduct autopsies. Coroner Clark found that Joan Herger was shot four times by a .38 caliber pistol. Two shots hit Joan in the left breast, one in the right breast, and one in the neck. Death was instantaneous. Vernon had one self-inflicted wound to his left temple. The .38 revolver was found still clutched in his left hand.

The authorities set out to inform the parents of the deceased youths. They first attempted to contact Mr. and Mrs. Herger, but found they were out of town in Springfield, Oregon. The Herger's, along with their younger son Joe, had been visiting their oldest son Mike, who was stationed in Springfield with the United States Army. The Herger's immediately headed back to Port Allegany.

Mr. and Mrs. Harold Thoren were also notified of their son's death, and they came to the funeral home to claim the remains. They were apprised that their son was the aggressor, and they were beyond shocked. Vernon's parents had his remains moved to the Gallup Funeral Home in Port Allegany to separate the funeral services.

Joan Herger was a local celebrity and considered to be one of the most expert horsewomen of North Western Pennsylvania for her riding ability. She had won numerous trophies and medals and, from 1937 to 1939, dominated the horse show events, which were held at the Bradford Valley Hunt Club. Joan's last appearance in a Valley Hunt Club horse show was in 1941. She was born in Port Allegany and had attended Port Allegany Schools. In her junior year, she had enrolled as a student at the Marymount School in Tarrytown, N. Y. and upon graduating there, she had entered William Smith College in Geneva, N. Y. In her third year at Geneva, she withdrew and returned to Port Allegany to work in a secretarial capacity at the North Penn Gas Company. Besides her parents, she was survived by two brothers, Mike and Joe, and one sister, Miss Carole Herger of Port Allegany. Joan was buried in the St. Gabriel Cemetery in Port Allegany.

Thoren graduated from Port Allegany High School in the class of 1940 and, after a short time, went to Buffalo, where he became employed at the Curtiss-Wright Plane Company. He worked there until returning to Port Allegany in the fall of 1942 to help his father on the family farm. He was survived by his parents, sisters, Miss Lenora Thoren and Miss Marilyn Thoren, and one brother Jene. Verne was buried in the McKean County Fairview Cemetery.

County Coroner Thomas Clark issued a statement that this was a murder-suicide with Thoren as the perpetrator. He also said there were no signs of a struggle and that no note was left. He said there would be no inquest as the case was "solved." Joan and Verne had been involved in a relationship since their days at the Port Allegany High School. Their relationship had become long-distance when Joan went to New York, and Joan eventually drifted away from the relationship. When both had returned to Port Allegany, they rekindled their relationship, but Joan wanted to pursue others and broke off the relationship. Thoren apparently had other ideas, and when he talked her into meeting him late at night in the park, he decided if he could not have her, no one would. What a tragic waste of two young lives.

Joan's grave in St. Gabriel's Cemetery.

Tarport

Hilton is buried in the Civil War section of Oak Hill Cemetery.

Tarport referred to the community centered at the corner of the Limestone and Kendall Creek roads. An undesirable citizen had reportedly been tarred and feathered there. A stranger was driving through the place one morning and seeing the act taking place, remarked that this must be a tar port. The name stuck and the area of the sixth ward of the City of Bradford is still sometimes referred to as Tarport. Tarport or "Kendall Creek" grew faster than any other part of the Tuna Valley. It had stores, a post office, and a large school. Tarport also had several undesirable houses within its midst, and one of these was the scene of a mysterious death in 1889. Was it a suicide or murder?

In a small one-story cottage located between the B. R. & O. and O. B. & W. railroad tracks lived an infamous lady, "Dutch" Annie Miller. Dutch Annie had moved to the Tarport area from Buffalo years before and had established a house of "ill repute" almost immediately. Annie welcomed men of all races to her "establishment," and her partner in this venture was a colored woman, Nora Richardson. Annie was known to take many lovers, but her established paramour was one William "Billy" Hilton. On the night of July 8th, 1889, this love-hate relationship took a turn for the worst.

Mr. Bat Conners was leaving the Miller cottage around 9 o'clock on that Monday evening when he heard a gunshot coming from the residence. Conners reentered the home and found the place in great confusion. The residents pointed to the back bedroom, and there Conners found a man he recognized as Billy Hilton in a dying condition. Conners saw Hilton had a wound in his groin area and blood flowing out in a steady stream. He ran out of the house and went to inform the authorities, while other occupants of the house began to scatter.

Police Chief McCrea and Constables Osborne and Fennerty were at the scene within minutes of being notified by Conners. They found what they described as a sickening sight. In a backroom used as a kitchen and sleeping apartment, lay the lifeless form of a well-known local character named Billy Hilton. The body lay on its back with the arms outstretched. His head was thrown back with its mouth open. The facial expression indicated suffering and horror. The officers removed a cloth that covered the left groin and exposed an ugly wound. The appearance of the wound indicated that it was made by a knife-like instrument. It was speculated that the wound had severed the main artery, and this had caused Hilton to bleed to death. On a table nearby lay a blood-stained knife. A bystander noted that the knife was used by Hilton to kill himself. The knife was reported to have been a common butter knife that was neither sharp nor pointed.

Constable Andy Evans arrived shortly, and Chief McCrea instructed him to place "Dutch" Annie Miller and her worker Nora Richardson under arrest, pending an investigation into Hilton's death. Both of the prisoners were placed in the local Tarport lockup.

Annie was interviewed in the jail, and she described Hilton as her "friend" who had visited her house that night and began an argument with an Italian named White, over White's attention to Annie. Hilton was a known lover of Annie, but it was also known that she shared her attentions with numerous lovers. Annie said Hilton went into the back room of the house and sat down by the kitchen table. Hilton called Annie to his side, and when she went into the room, Hilton had blood flowing from a wound in his groin he had apparently administered himself. Annie said she called her roommate, Nora Richardson, into the room and told her to go and fetch a doctor. She said Billy then fell over onto the floor and called to her "Annie" and died. When questioned on the gunshot that had been heard in her house, Annie was very contradictory in her statements and then said there had been no gunshot, but the noise that was heard was firecrackers.

Nora was interviewed, and her story was similar to Annie's, but she mentioned additional men who were present during the incident. Nora said that a man named Casily and a man named Siaton were present and saw the incident take place. Nora denied that any gunshot had taken place. A search was then conducted for the men who were named as witnesses. Coroner Heffner took charge of the case and arranged an inquest to investigate the death of Billy Hilton.

The body of Billy Hilton was removed to the Otto Koch Undertaking Rooms on Mechanic Street for a formal autopsy. An examination of the remains was made by Doctors McCarty, Rae, and Johnston. The autopsy found that the femoral artery had been severed. The wound, while plausibly made by the butter knife, did not appear to have been self-inflicted. When a flattened bullet was found deeper in the wound, the direction of the investigation took a different path.

Dutch Annie, who had told numerous contradictory stories, once again changed her story when confronted with the finding of the bullet.

Annie now testified at the inquest that she shot Hilton, who was in an intoxicated state, and when he continued to threaten to kill her, she had stabbed him. Annie said she had done this in self-defense. The medical professionals said that the gunshot to Hilton had not severed the artery but that the knife wound inflicted afterward had. Annie was reportedly changing her story as more medical evidence was presented. The coroner's jury then determined that William Hilton had come to his death at the hands of "Dutch" Annie Miller from a gunshot wound followed by a knife wound. Annie was formally charged with the first-degree murder of Hilton and taken to the county jail in Smethport to await a trial in front of a grand jury.

William "Billy" Hilton came to Bradford from Lockport, New York, roughly eleven years before his death. His mother still resided in Lockport and was notified of his untimely death. Hilton was around forty-six years of age. He had become Annie's lover months before his death and had a reputation in Bradford and Tarport as living a dissolute life and was known to carouse with unsavory characters. He also reportedly lived off of Annie's wages from her sinful operation. Locals said that when he had arrived in Bradford, he was known as an industrious and trustworthy worker. He had eventually succumbed to alcohol and the unsavory life which often comes with overindulgence. On Wednesday morning, Mrs. Hilton sent word to Bradford that her son should be buried in Bradford, and his body was moved to a vacant building in Oak Hill Cemetery, where it reposed during the night. On Thursday morning, owing to Hilton having been a veteran of the civil war, the Grand Army of the Republic conducted services. He was interred there, and his gravesite continues to be honored with a flag due to his service to the country.

The trial of Annie Miller commenced in Smethport on October 9th, 1889. District Attorney Sturgeon, assisted by Attorney Cotter, prosecuted the case for the Commonwealth while Attorney Mullin represented the defense. Judge T. A. Morrison presided. The jury chosen included John A. Evans, William H. Cazwell, J. H. Dawson, J.

H. Leroy, W. D. Thomas, James Leak, Ike Baker, W. W. Chaffee, and John H. Sellen.

The prosecution called Nora Anderson to the stand. Nora testified she was at the house on the night of July 8th and that William Hilton, Andy Casily, Bat Conners, John Siaton and Billy White were also there. She said Hilton was very drunk and quarreling with Annie. Hilton had run out of the back door and barged in the front door and threw a cat at Annie, and then went into the bedroom and laid on the bed. Annie sent Bat in to tell him to leave, and Bat came out and said, "He has a knife!" Annie went into the room, and they began to quarrel again. Hilton had come out of the bedroom and said he was going to bed, and Annie locked the bedroom door behind him. She said Hilton had punched the door, and she heard a shot. She said she saw Hilton stagger, and she ran out. She did not see Annie shoot as her back was to her. She said she knew Annie had a gun under her apron. When they ran outside after she heard the shot, Annie had come to the door and said, "come back in, I did not shoot him, I shot at the door." Annie told Nora that Hilton had cut himself and that she should go and get a doctor. Nora said she went and got Dr. McCarty, and he came and examined Hilton. Annie told the doctor that Hilton had stabbed himself with a knife and gave him a *Case* knife which was covered with blood. Nora said she saw cotton on the wound and that Hilton's pants were pushed back from the injury. Annie had been trying to stop the flow of blood. On cross-examination, Nora said she only heard one shot. Nora then said she had known Hilton for about a year. She had never talked to him as she was afraid of him. She first saw Hilton that night at around 4 or 5. Nora was in the house when Annie saw Hilton coming up the street. She said she told Annie, here comes your man, and Annie said, let us go and hide from him. Hilton wildly ran in the front door and Annie ran out the back door. Hilton followed her and was so drunk he fell upon the railroad tracks adjacent to the house. Nora testified that both Annie and Hilton came back into the house and were fighting. Hilton called Annie bad names and threatened to strike her. Annie ordered Hilton to leave her house and also called him foul names. Hilton told Bat Conners that if he tried to sleep with Annie that night he would be sorry. Annie and Hilton then went into the back room and continued to quarrel, and Annie came out of the backroom and said Hilton had a bread knife in his hand. Annie had marks upon her neck and arms and all over her body.

Bat Connors was the next to testify. He said he was at Annie's house at around 9 o'clock that evening and was drinking beer. When he was leaving and walking down the street, he heard a gunshot. He said he went back into the house and asked Annie what was going on. Annie told him nothing, and then he looked into the back room and saw Hilton on the floor. He believed Hilton was dying then. Annie never mentioned anything about a gun while he was there. Connors said he then went up the street to inform the authorities. While at the police station, he heard another shot, which would have been twenty-five minutes after the first shot. On cross-examination, he said he was there from 7 0'clock until 9 o'clock drinking beer. He heard a racket in the bedroom, did hear Annie mention that Hilton had a knife. He said he opened the bedroom door and told them to stop fighting. He did not see Hilton hit Annie, nor did he see Hilton throw a cat at Annie. Hilton had asked him earlier if he was Annie's lover and that Hilton was quite intoxicated that night.

Andrew Casily testified next. He said he went to Annie's house about a half-hour before the shooting. Hilton arrived drunk and went to break open the bedroom door. Casily heard a shot and saw a flash between the door and the stove. He said Annie was standing there. Before this, he saw Hilton trying to force the door and heard Hilton say, "Gentlemen, I am going to bed." Annie said, "You will not go to bed in there!" He ran out of the house when he heard the shot. Annie came out and told the men to come back in and that she had shot no one and had only shot at the door. Casily went back in and found Hilton lying on the floor. He said Annie told him he fell on his knife. He said he saw no revolver. On cross-examination, he said that Hilton and Annie were quarreling the whole time he was at their house. He said he heard a scuffle in the bedroom, and someone said he had a knife. He said he heard Annie scream and say Hilton had grabbed her nose.

Coroner Heffner then testified as to his involvement in the case. He produced a pistol that was found behind Miller's house the day after the shooting. When Heffner was questioned about statements Annie had made in front of the coroner's inquest, the defense objected. After an argument of over two hours of why these statements should not be admissible, the judge agreed with the defense and ruled that statements Annie had made at the inquest could not be introduced into the trial. Attorney Cotter then switched to the testimony that Heffner had solicited from Annie the day after the shooting when she was in the local lockup. Mullin once again objected, but this time the judge allowed Heffner to testify. Heffner testified that Annie said she and Hilton were quarreling and that she fired the revolver low and hit him in the leg. That Hilton was sitting in a chair when she fired. When he questioned her on how Hilton had received the cut, she said she did not know, he may have fallen on it and that he had a knife. Annie told Heffner she had shot Hilton with a revolver that he had given her two weeks before the incident. She said she threw it out back of the house after the shooting, where it was found the next day. He also identified a quite common looking *Case* knife with bloodstains on it as the one he discovered at Annie's on the night of the murder. Heffner then identified the flattened bullet that Dr. Rae had cut out of Hilton's body. Heffner also testified that when he got to the house on the night of the murder, he found Hilton lying dead in a pool of blood. Hilton was partially undressed. He found Hilton's pants undone, and when examining the fatal wound, he said it appeared to have been a knife wound.

Chief of Police McCrea then testified he was present when Annie spoke to the coroner. He said he heard her say she shot Hilton in self-defense, that he was sitting on a chair when she shot him and that she did not know how he was cut. She repeated to him that she shot in self-defense and had no idea how he was cut.

Dr. McCartey followed immediately and testified to the findings of his autopsy and said he found the bullet about one and a half inches below the cut. He stated that the knife wound had severed the artery. He noted that he did not find a bullet hole in the pants. The Commonwealth then concluded the case for the prosecution.

Attorney Mullin then opened the case for the defense. He outlined the theory that the shot was fired in self-defense; that Hilton was in Annie's house and had no business being there. He refused to leave; he choked Annie, beat her, threatened her life, and compelled her to give him money for liquor. Hilton was drunk and quarrelsome that night, and she believed she was in danger. The defense further would prove that the bullet fired by Annie never went into the body of Hilton and that the one found by Dr. Rae had been in Hilton's body for years.

Mrs. Moss, a neighbor of Annie's, testified first. She said she had spoken with Hilton about a month before the shooting and that he had told her he did not care about Annie and only wanted to use her for money. Mrs. Moss questioned him why he stayed with her, and Hilton replied that if she is damn fool enough to keep me, let her do it. When Moss was questioned about Hilton and Annie fighting, this was objected to by the Commonwealth, and the objection was sustained by the judge. The defense was attempting to show that Hilton assaulted Annie regularly and that her life was in danger.

Alderman Wolcott testified next that on June 15th, Hilton was arrested on a charge of assault and battery and threats to kill on allegations made by Annie Miller. Wolcott said that previous to this incident, Hilton was charged with the same charges filed by Annie. Hilton pled guilty to the charges of assault and battery in the previous case but denied the threats.

Alice Grey testified that she had visited Annie's house that past April. While she was there, she saw Hilton knock Annie into a corner and then kick her. She overheard Hilton say if he got ahold of her, he would kill her. Grey said she left with Annie, and they went and filed charges that resulted in Hilton's arrest.

Ms. Eva Hart then testified that about three weeks before Hilton died, she saw him on the street. Hilton was pretty drunk. Hilton told Hart that he was going home to Annie's and that he was going to lick her until she was afraid to nose around about him.

Andy Evans testified that he was called to Annie's several times because of Hilton. Hilton had come and asked him to accompany him to Annie's to get his clothes. Hilton said he had quarreled with Annie and wanted his clothes to go away to Buffalo. Evans went with Hilton to Annie's where she packed his clothes into two suitcases. He heard Hilton say to Annie, "you damn bitch, I ought to strangle you!" Evans told him to calm down. Annie told Hilton that if you are going to Buffalo, you will need some money. She knew he had none and had never known him to have any money. Annie told Hilton that if he went to Buffalo and stayed there and did not bother her again, she would give him $5. Annie gave him the money, but Hilton never went to Buffalo.

Charles Olin testified that one day he was walking along the railroad tracks behind Annie's house and saw Annie run out of her house and then heard a pistol shot. Annie came to him and wanted him to go with her to her home. He objected, but Annie insisted, and he did accompany her. Hilton was standing in the doorway with his hand under his coat. Hilton said he would kill the damn bitch if she did not behave. Olin told him not to do that, and Hilton put his pistol into his pocket.

Minnie Kelly testified that she boarded with Annie and had heard Hilton say he would kill Annie. She said Hilton quarreled with Annie often and said he would kill her regularly. Hilton also threw beer bottles at Annie.

The defense then called Dr. Freeman, who said he was an expert in gunshot wounds. Freeman said that a bullet fired into Hilton would have severed the artery, and death would have been instant. Freeman also said that if Hilton suffered a fresh gunshot wound, the knife wound would not have been able to obliterate the evidence of the gunshot, such as was the case at present. The doctor was shown the bullet, and he said the appearance of the bullet gave him the impression that it was in the body of Hilton for a long time due to the polished effect. He said the polished effect could have come from rubbing against the muscles for an extended period. He was shown the pistol allegedly used in the shooting and said the barrel had five grooves in it, and the bullet taken from Hilton had six, which showed it could not have come from this pistol. Freeman then had two scales brought in and put the bullet taken out of Hilton on one side and placed an unfired .32 caliber slug on the other side. The bullet taken from Hilton was heavier, which Freeman said should not have been true. In his opinion, the bullet found in Hilton was not fired by the pistol in evidence.

The defense then called J. Contril, a pension agent. Contril said that on the 7th or 8th of July, Hilton had told him he was going to apply for a military pension due to a bullet he was carrying from the war. The prosecution objected to this evidence and said the witness was never on the list of potential witnesses and that his testimony was never introduced before and should be thrown out. The defense said this would prove that Hilton had a bullet in his leg before the incident. Judge Morrison agreed with the prosecution, and the testimony of Contril was excluded from the record. The defense then rested.

In rebuttal, the prosecution called M. J. Hadley, who was a practicing gunsmith for ten years. Hadley testified that he had examined the bullet taken out of the body of Hilton and found five grooves, the same amount he found in the murder weapon.

Dr. McCartey was recalled and testified that in his opinion, the bullet taken from Hilton's body was only in the body a short time as it was not encysted. McCartey said that he had fired bullets into a shank bone of beef from six feet away. He showed the bullets to the jury and explained that a bullet was encysted when a membrane had grown around it.

Dr. Wells then testified and brought a powerful microscope with him. He explained when he examined the bullet taken from Hilton's body; he found gunpowder crystals still attached to the bullet. He found the same crystals attached to the bullets fired into the beef shank. He said he would not expect to find the crystals in a bullet that had been in a body for a lengthy period. He also said the bullet that came out of Hilton was shiny and that he would expect a bullet to be much darker if it had been in a body for a lengthy period of time. The prosecution then rested.

The defense then made an impassioned plea to the jury. Annie was an abused woman who had been repeatedly threatened by William Hilton. On the night of the shooting, Hilton had physically assaulted Annie and had threatened her life. Annie had shot at Hilton in self-defense, and her bullet had struck the door to the bedroom. The bullet found in Hilton was an old war wound and had nothing to do with his death. Hilton had cut himself with the knife that he had previously wielded to threaten Annie and had unfortunately bled to death.

The prosecution closed with the facts that Annie admitted she had shot a revolver towards Hilton. The bullet had struck Hilton in the groin area, and Annie, whether in an attempt to remove the bullet or kill Hilton, had knifed him in the area where he had been shot. Annie caused the death of Hilton and deserved to be found guilty of murder in the first-degree.

Judge Morrison charged the jury and told them they could convict Annie on first-degree murder, second-degree murder, manslaughter, or acquittal, and they left to deliberate at 2:12 pm on October 11th, 1889. As Annie was led back to the jail to await her verdict, she was overheard muttering, "All that is left now is to put the rope around my neck." The jury signaled they had reached a verdict at 5:30 pm, and Annie was brought from the jail into the courtroom. The jury found Annie guilty of murder in the second-degree, where the maximum penalty was twelve years in the penitentiary. Annie sobbed when she was returned to the jail and at once fell ill, delaying her sentencing until Thursday afternoon the following week.

The court convened once again on Thursday, October 17th, and defense attorney Mullin made an argument in favor of a new trial for his client. Judge Morrison denied this request and asked Annie if she had anything to say why sentence should not be passed upon her.

In very broken English, Annie said: "You Honor, I did shoot, but I did not intend to kill him, and I don't think I did. He was sitting on a chair, and when I came in, he rose and said, Annie, I am going to kill you. I was so scared and frightened. I shot to frighten him off. He had a bullet in his leg; he said he was going to get a pension. One day I felt the bullet in his leg. I did not intend to kill him." Judge Morrison told the prisoner that she had been well defended by skillful counsel and that the jury had been merciful, sparing her from the first-degree murder conviction. He then sentenced her to confinement in the Western Penitentiary at separate and solitary confinement for eleven years and ten months. This sentence brought a flood of tears from Annie, and she looked forlorn and friendless as she clutched the jail warden's arm as he was leading her to her cell. It was observed at the time that her appearance had changed drastically from when she was originally arrested. Then she was described as being bloated with a spotty complexion, no doubt as a result of her wicked ways. At her sentencing, she was described as having a clear complexion and had lost a significant amount of weight. Annie was around forty-five years old when she entered the penitentiary. Annie was described as the model of a reformed citizen during her time at the penitentiary, and an application was made in October 1897 for a pardon. Annie was pardoned and left the penitentiary, said to be over fifty years of age, and in declining health. The whereabouts of Annie after her release are not known.

An early view of Tarport.

Death In Clermont

The Clermont Brick Plant.

Today Clermont is a sleepy little hamlet with few signs of the once-bustling community that existed in the past. One of the largest employers back in 1913, the Clermont Brick Plant, was a massive enterprise that operated twenty-four hours and three hundred sixty-five days a year. Personnel were always on the job. Another large employer in the area was the United National Gas Company which had an office in Clermont. The gas company had many employees throughout the area who worked the natural gas deposits that were being discovered almost daily. The need for numerous employees to complete the physical needs of these industries brought many men, both natives and foreigners to the area to fill these positions. The different nationalities and upbringings often caused fights and misunderstandings due to the language barrier. What happened in 1913 was a combination of both a language barrier and another ignored calamity among people those days, mental illness.

John Gallagher was thirty-two years old in 1913 and an ambitious man. Gallagher, who had resided in Emporium with his family, had set out from his home in search of employment. He had success at the

United National Gas Company offices in Clermont. Gallagher had been hired as a laborer on the pipelines and was stationed at the Betula pump station. Gallagher would still have to travel to Clermont to receive his pay and supplies, but generally, he worked around the clock in Betula. Payday for Gallagher was every other Thursday, and he would draw his pay in Clermont. He would then wire money to support his mother in Emporium. On Thursday afternoon, August 7, 1913, Gallagher and a companion set out on the trek from Betula to Clermont. Gallagher's companion was in search of work while Gallagher was expecting to draw his pay. Along the way to Clermont, the companion got word of an available job on the Shawmut line and left to follow up on the lead, which was located towards Crosby. Gallagher continued to Clermont and promptly went to the gas company office. He unfortunately missed the paymaster that day and realized he would have to spend the night in Clermont. There was a social gathering in Clermont that evening, and Gallaher stopped and observed the dancing and partying; however, he did not take part in the celebration. It was now late in the evening, and Gallagher went to the Clermont House to see if he could secure a room for the evening. Finding the hotel closed for the night, he did not know where he would spend the night. A man near the hotel pointed towards the large Clermont Sewer Pipe Plant and said that the boiler room in the back of the building would be a warm place to bed down for the night. Gallagher accepted this man's recommendation and walked towards the plant. As he was walking through the plant towards the boiler room, he passed the kilns. Two employees of the plant were working there and at once confronted Gallagher. The taller male told Gallagher that the plant was private property and that he had best retreat and not show his face in this area again. Gallagher apologized and turned to walk back the way he had come. Three loud gunshots then shattered the stillness of the night. The first two shots went wild, but the third struck Gallagher in the right hip and traveled through his body, exiting near his navel. Gallagher slumped to the ground and realized he was seriously wounded. He turned around to see who had fired the gun, but the two employees had disappeared. Gallagher then saw the plant superintendent's house in the distance and holding his stomach; he made his way to the house.

Gallagher began banging loudly on the front door and roused W. E. Ringrose, the superintendent of the plant. Ringrose opened his door and found Gallagher seated on a chair on his porch, crying out in pain. His cries for help had alerted several other gentlemen who were walking nearby, and they also appeared on the porch. The men gathered up Gallagher and carried him to the Clermont House, where the local physician, Dr. Mausery, kept his office. Dr. Mausery was awoken and began to examine Gallagher. Dr. Mausery quickly determined that the wound could very well cause death and disclosed this to the injured Gallagher. Gallagher asked to see a priest, and the local Catholic priest, Father Carpenter, was summoned. Father Carpenter administered the last rights to Gallagher while Mausery set up transportation to try to get Gallagher to a hospital in an attempt to save his life. While waiting for the automobile to arrive, Gallagher told Dr. Mausery of his confrontation at the clay plant and how two men had accosted him. He described the tall man as the one whom he believed had fired the rounds.

At around five in the morning, Earl Flickinger arrived with his automobile, and Gallagher, accompanied by Dr. Mausery, both entered the vehicle for the thirty-five-mile ride to the Ridgway Hospital. The trio reached the hospital at 6:30 am. Gallagher was deemed too weak to attempt surgery, and he was sedated in the hope that his condition would improve. Gallagher's condition continued to weaken, and he sadly expired at 9:30 that morning.

McKean County Detective E. W. Jones was notified and made a hasty trip to Clermont from his residence in Smethport. Jones spoke to the men who had transported Gallagher to the hotel and quickly went to the clay plant to search for suspects. He arrested two men, Christi Pete and Tony Lazzo, who were working the graveyard shift the previous night. The men matched the descriptions that Gallagher had supplied. Jones had the men transported to the Smethport jail for further interrogation and were then held on suspicion of attempted murder. Jones was later notified of Gallagher's death and knew he would be upgrading the charges to murder, pending the results of a coroner's inquest that would be held in Clermont on Saturday morning.

McKean County Coroner Sherman had requested that the Van Aiken Funeral Home in Ridgway ship Gallagher's body in ice on Friday evening directly to Smethport, so an autopsy could be performed while the body was still fresh. For unknown reasons, the funeral director ignored this message and instead kept the body unrefrigerated and sent the body on Saturday morning. When the body arrived, it was in what was described as a horrible condition. On Saturday afternoon, Doctors McCoy and Hamilton performed an autopsy at Specht and Sasse's Morgue.

Coroner Sherman empaneled an inquest on Saturday morning in Smethport, consisting of Oscar Engstrom, S. E. Bell, C. L. Irons, L. K. Hogarth, A. A Hazen and U. H. Foote. The jury then went to the morgue and viewed the body of Gallagher before retreating to the courthouse library to hear evidence in the case.

Dr. E. A. Mausery, the physician who attended Gallagher on the morning of the shooting, was called first. He said he was called to attend to the wounded man between the hours of one and two in the morning on Friday. He found the man on the hotel porch and had him carried up the stairs to his office, where he examined the wound. The bullet had entered the right hip and he was of the opinion that the ball lodged by the navel. Dr. Mausery stated that Gallagher had told him he had walked to Clermont from Betula and that he intended to return to Betula to go to work Friday morning. He said he found the hotel closed and decided to go to the sewer pipe plant to spend the night. He told the doctor that he was accosted by a tall man with a mustache accompanied by a shorter younger man. The tall man ordered him to leave the property, and this is the one that shot him. The doctor said that he considered Gallagher to be in fair shape when he first examined him. When he probed the wound further, he decided that the wound was potentially fatal. He told Gallagher that he only had one chance in a thousand to survive his injury. Gallagher asked for a priest, and after the session with the priest, Dr. Mausery went with Gallagher to the Ridgway Hospital. Gallagher was in a very weakened condition upon arrival at the Ridgway Hospital and was unable to have surgery and he eventually succumbed to his injuries.

Mr. Earl Flickinger, the man who used his car to transport Gallagher to the Ridgway Hospital, was called next. Flickinger related that Gallagher had told him how he went to find shelter at the tile works and that two men had confronted him and ordered him to leave the premises. The taller man was the one who had shot him, and he had never met the man before. Flickinger said that when he started away from Clermont in his automobile, Gallagher bade farewell to all of the bystanders and said he probably would never return, which turned out to be true.

W. A. Hovis was sworn. He said he was a foreman at Clermont with the United Gas Company. He said he talked with Gallagher at the Clermont House at around 2:30 in the morning on that fateful night. He said Gallagher was in much pain and did not know the man who shot him, only that he was a tall man. Gallagher asked Hovis to get a priest as he did not think he would live, and Hovis did summon a priest.

W. E. Ringross, Superintendent of the Clermont Sewer Pipe Plant, was sworn next. He said he was awakened by shots and saw a man coming up the street crying in pain. The man came to his door and knocked loudly. When he opened the door, he found the man sitting on a chair, and when he saw he was injured, he yelled for help, and several men appeared and carried Gallagher in the chair to the Clermont House where the doctor resided.

D. H. Sullivan was called, and he testified that he was employed in the boiler house of the sewer plant. He said he was awakened by gunshots on that Friday morning and went outside to investigate. He said Christi Pete and Tony Lazzo were working at the kilns that night, and he went and asked them what had happened. Pete replied that he did not hear any shots and did not know what Sullivan was talking about. He said four men were working that night at the plant: himself, John Shilia the night watchman, and Pete and Lazzo at the kilns.

Mr. Ringross was recalled. In answer to a question by District Attorney Wilson, Ringross confirmed that he had given orders not to allow loafers about the tile works, but that he certainly did not imply that trespassers should be shot.

John Shilia, the night watchman, was called next. Due to his limited understanding of the English language, he was unable to answer most questions. He did say that he was asleep in the boiler room with Sullivan when he was awakened by gunshots. He and Sullivan went to investigate and talked with Pete, who denied hearing any shots.

After hearing all of the evidence, the jury rendered a verdict that John Gallagher came to his death on the morning of August 8, 1913, from a bullet wound fired by someone unknown to the jury.

Immediately following the coroner's inquest, a hearing took place in front of Justice Gleason regarding the arrest of Christi Pete and Tony Lazzo on suspicion of having a hand in the murder of John Gallagher. District Attorney Wilson examined the witnesses, which included Dr. Mausery, Earl Flickinger, W. A. Hovis, D. H. Sullivan, and John Shilia, who all had just testified at the coroner's inquest. Mr. Hovis only added that Gallagher had told him that the person who shot him was tall with a mustache.

Dr. McCoy, one of the physicians who performed the autopsy, testified that the shot had entered Gallagher's hip, shattering the pelvic bone and gone through the body. The bullet passed through the large intestines near the appendix. The bullet was not found and had passed through the body. Death was due to shock caused by the bullet wound.

After hearing all of the evidence, Justice Gleason held Christi Pete without bail for his appearance at the next term of criminal court. Tony Lazzo was released from jail.

John Gallagher was born and raised in Emporium. His father had died young, and Gallagher supported his mother and one sister Margaret who still resided at home in Emporium. He also had a married sister, Mrs. P. A. Coffey of Limestone, New York, and one brother, P. H. Gallagher of Franklin, PA. All of Gallagher's family gathered in Smethport on Saturday and decided to hold his funeral and burial there on Sunday afternoon. Funeral services were conducted at the St. Elizabeth Roman Catholic Church in Smethport on Sunday afternoon, and burial took place in St. Elizabeth's Cemetery.

Christi "Big Pete" Pete was born in Macedonia and emigrated to this country in the earlier part of the 1900s. Pete had ended up in McKean County, working at various industries that were in desperate need of physical labor. Christi was a somewhat violent and unpredictable character who had been in trouble with the law before the incident in Clermont. In 1909 he was involved in a fight in Crosby and had disemboweled a man with a bread knife. The man survived, and the only sentence Christi received was a three-month term in the county jail after being convicted of assault and battery. He was suspected of doing the shooting of Gallagher because he and Lazzo were the only two working at the kilns the night of the shooting, and he matched the description of the shooter. Christi also said he heard no shots, even though the shooting had taken place at the kilns. Christi denied shooting Gallagher but refused to answer any questions during his arrest or subsequent interrogations. While Christi was incarcerated awaiting trial, the jail warden noticed many bizarre behaviors from Christi. These included loud conversations with himself, walking around naked in his cell, and refusal to follow even the most basic commands. Christi also self-mutilated his body, which resulted in many scars and bleeding wounds that required medical attention. As the criminal court session neared, the warden consulted the district attorney and the defense attorney about his suspicions. A session with Dr. Mitchell, Superintendent of the Warren State Hospital was arranged, assisted by Dr. Chadwick for the defense. Both doctors concluded that Christi was unbalanced mentally. A special criminal court hearing took place on December 8, 1913, in front of a jury with Judge Joseph Bouton presiding. Testimony was taken from Sheriff Bain, Detective Jones, Captain Webb, and Doctors Mitchell and Chadwick. After hearing the evidence, the jury pronounced Christi insane and recommended that he be committed to the Warren State Hospital for an indeterminate amount of time. In the event he became rational again, he was to be brought back to McKean County for trial on the murder charge. While awaiting transfer to Warren, Christi went on a hunger strike and refused to eat for over a week. After being force fed and regaining his strength, he was transferred to Warren. At the hospital he was described as reacting to treatment, but never was considered sane again. Pete never returned to face the murder charges in McKean County, and it is assumed he spent his final days at Warren State Hospital.

Gallagher is buried in St. Elizabeth's Cemetery in Smethport.

A Clear Case of Suicide

Annie Peeler with a bandage on her forehead where she was "injured."

The most common motives for murder are love, lust, loathing, and loot, or so say the criminalists. Jealousy fits into both love and lust, and when that love is unrequited, loathing then becomes applicable. The news stories today are full of murders where one partner kills another because they caught the partner cheating. In 1908 such a case happened in Bradford, which encompassed three of the four most common motives. Was this incident an attempted murder-suicide or was it a thinly veiled coverup for a cold-blooded murder? This case, while settled in the courts at the time, remains an open verdict as far as I am concerned.

Roy Warner was born in Lock Haven in 1884 to Mr. and Mrs. Curzey Warner of Brookville. He had interned as a barber at a local shop in Brookville. When Roy heard of an opening at Kramer Brothers

Barbershop on Mechanic Street in Bradford in 1906, he traveled to the city and promptly joined the business. Roy, who was tall, lean and handsome, found himself becoming lonely after spending long days at the barbershop. He began to frequent the saloons and bars in search of a companion. At one local watering hole, he met Anna Peeler, a rather rough and frequent bar patron who already had an unsavory reputation in the community. Roy quickly fell in love with Anna, who, while not a physical beauty, did possess some attractive personality traits. Anna made Roy laugh and he no longer had to spend his evenings alone. In a short time, the pair moved in with each other at a rooming house located at the rear of 23 Davis Street. Roy professed his love for Anna, and the couple talked of marriage in the future. Harmony, however, was not to be a part of this relationship. Anna continued to prowl the local nightspots almost every night, and Roy, who worked nearly every day but Sunday, was too tired to accompany her. He pleaded with Anna to stay at home with him, but Anna, who was fiercely independent, refused to be contained. Neighbors in adjoining rooms often heard the couple in loud arguments, and objects crashed into the walls during these altercations. Roy was insanely jealous of Anna. He often woke up during the night and found her not at home. He would prowl the local joints in search of her and usually found her sitting at a bar surrounded by men buying her drinks and enjoying her attentions. Roy told her he would not put up with this behavior and that if she did not change, he was leaving forever. This precarious situation continued for two years, culminating in a final fight on Sunday afternoon, August 2nd, 1908.

On Saturday night, August 1st, Roy and Anna had another of their infamous arguments. Roy had found a letter that Anna was writing to a suiter in Buffalo, New York, and he questioned Anna on her intentions. Anna told him that she had been writing to this gentleman for several weeks and that yes, indeed, this man had romantic intentions for her. This caused a loud fight, which all of the neighbors heard. The landlord, Mr. Sam Mooney, had entered their room and told them that if they did not cease this constant fighting, he would have to evict them and call the police. Roy and Anna apologized, and Mr. Mooney invited the pair to visit his room on Sunday night to discuss a party he was planning. The pair apologized to Mr. Mooney and laid upon their bed to rest and discuss their differences. After talking for a while and apologizing to each other, Roy fell asleep. Anna, never one to retire early, went out on the town by herself and once again enjoyed the company of strange men at the area bars which were packed on this weekend night. Roy woke up during the night and found that Anna was no longer by his side. He seethed with anger and was waiting when she came through the door early on Sunday morning.

Roy and Anna immediately began to argue, with Anna on the defensive. Anna said she had spent the night with her good friend Nancy and that nothing nefarious had happened. She said she woke up at midnight and could not rouse Roy to go out with her and had left to visit Nancy. The arguing continued for quite some time until Mr. Mooney knocked on their door and told them they needed to quiet it down. Anna promised Mr. Mooney they would be quiet, and the only sound coming from their room after that was hushed whispers.

Roy left the apartment and proceeded to a room he had just rented in the fourth ward. Roy was planning on leaving Anna once and for all. He was seen by locals carrying his belongings along the street and spoke to several, telling them that he was done with Anna and from now on would live on his own.

A certain George Fagnan had recently died, and his funeral was being held on that Sunday afternoon. Both Roy and Anna were close friends of Fagnan, and both attended in their Sunday best. The pair were observed standing together on Main Street as the funeral procession passed heading towards the cemetery. After the funeral they were noticed to leave together walking in the direction of their Davis Street apartment.

At around 4:30 in the afternoon, four shots were heard coming from the room of Anna and Roy, and the residents of the rooming house gathered in the hallway. Ms. Blanche Myers entered Anna's room and was met at once by Anna, who exclaimed, "Roy has shot me and killed himself!" Other tenants now appeared in the room, and the authorities were notified. The police arrived to find Roy deceased and Anna with several bleeding wounds. Anna said that she and Roy were lying on her bed and discussing Roy's extreme jealously. Anna said she explained to Roy that she was not being unfaithful and never had been. She said Roy had said to her that if he found out she was with another man; he would kill them both. Anna was reading the *Buffalo Sunday Paper* while they laid in bed and Roy was staring at the ceiling. Unexpectedly, Roy said "There!" and pulled out a revolver with his left hand and shot Anna in her temple. Anna said she was temporarily unconscious and did not see Roy shoot himself. Warner's body laid neatly dressed on the bed while Anna told her story. Pools of blood were forming both about his head and below his heart, where there were two obvious wounds. The pistol lay on his right side. An ambulance was sent to take Anna to the hospital while the authorities arranged for the body of Warner to be taken to a local funeral parlor for an autopsy.

Anna walked on her own to the awaiting ambulance, and the attendants could see that the bullet wounds to her body were not serious. She could be heard joking with the attendants and was quickly taken to the hospital. Bradford Police Chief Murray, after viewing the body of Warner and speaking with Anna, immediately believed that this incident might not have been as Anna had explained. He thought the death might have been a murder committed by Peeler. Murray sent word to the hospital that Peeler was not to be released from the hospital but taken into police custody when and if she was released from medical care. Murray also informed the district attorney and county detective of his initial suspicions, and they both headed to Bradford.

Coroner Sherman, realizing this was not a clear case of suicide, empaneled a jury to hear the evidence. Sherman chose: F. W. Winger as foreman, J. B. Fox, L. W. Oakes, Ellis Werthman, Mose Cohn, and

Delos Armstrong as the jury. The jury viewed the body of Warner, and Dr. Walker disclosed the two distinct bullet wounds that Warner suffered and explained either of them would have been fatal.

Adelbert Walker was sworn in. He was a good friend of Warner and was with him on the Sunday afternoon before his death. He said Warner told him he was moving to Mrs. Brown's house that day and that he was done with Anna. Warner told him that they had fought all weekend and that Anna had a violent temper. Warner had to restrain Peeler's arms to keep her from striking him. Warner told Walker that he had never struck a woman. Warner also said that Peeler had told him that if he left her, he would pay for it.

The jury next swore in Ms. Blanche Myers, who testified as to what she had witnessed and what Anna had told her immediately after the shooting. Myers added that the couple had been together for a long time and that they both appeared to be extremely jealous of each other, and she had often heard Warner tell Anna to take no notice of any other young men. She also said she had observed considerable quarreling between the two.

Sam Mooney, the landlord, testified next. Mooney said he had broken up a loud argument between the two on Saturday night which he stated was a regular occurrence. Mooney said that he heard Warner tell Anna that if she continued to anger Roy, she would regret it. Mooney said Roy did not say how she would regret it, only making the idle threat. He told the couple that unless they quieted down, he would call the police and have them evicted. Mooney identified the murder weapon as belonging to himself. He said he kept it in a drawer full of odds and ends and had no idea how it ended up in the couple's apartment but had shown both of them its location previously.

The jury then went to the hospital to take Anna's statement for the record. Anna testified that she lived with Warner but was not married to him. She said she went to the Fagnan funeral on Sunday. Warner accompanied her. Warner was taking things from their room to Mrs.

Brown's on that Sunday morning prior to the funeral. Both had returned to their shared room after the funeral to discuss Roy's intentions. Anna said she laid down on the bed with her feet towards the door. Warner laid beside her right side. She said she was reading a newspaper, and Warner said "There!" and placed the revolver at her head and fired. She said the pistol was in Roy's left hand. She said when she regained consciousness, she jumped up quickly and found he had shot himself. His undershirt was burning. When he placed the gun at her head, she said, "What are you doing?" "We had had quarrels." "The only word that he spoke was "There." Ann said she was twenty-two years old, and Roy was twenty-three. She said she previously lived in Lewis Run and had never been married. "I don't know in which place he shot himself first. I did not know where Mr. Mooney kept his gun. He pulled the gun; I don't know from where. Warner was lying on his back, and as he shot, I turned just as the gun was fired." When questioned about the quarrels, she said she had been writing a letter to a friend in Buffalo. "He asked me if I was going to mail it?" I said, "yes.' He asked me if I heard from my Buffalo friend. I said, "yes.' I said I have been hearing from him for three weeks. "Why didn't you let me know before?" he asked. "None of your business," said I.

"We argued and quarreled Saturday night and were told to stop by Mr. Mooney." "Saturday night, we had another argument." The witness showed where she had been bruised on her arms. "He tried to bite my cheek."

"When I was out evenings, he would come and look for me. He had said that he would never leave me while I was alive. I had known him for over two years and had no other lover. We were both lying on two pillows, one on top of the other. My dress was burning around the hole where he had shot me. His clothing was also burning about his breast. I reached over and put out the fire." I picked up a bullet at the foot of the bed. I picked up the revolver and "broke" it and placed the bullet in the weapon. I did that after I had told Ms. Meyers what had happened. I then placed the gun on the bed where I had found it on

Roy's right side. I don't know whether he was breathing or not. I opened the revolver to see how many shots had been fired." When questioned why she opened the gun, she said she didn't know. She also said Warner had a quick temper and she told him she was going to leave. She said Warner told her "not alive!"

Dr. J. B. Stewart, who performed the autopsy on the body of Warner, was the next witness to testify. Stewart stated that he had found that a bullet had entered the body between the fourth and fifth ribs on the left side of the chest directly below the nipple. It had pierced the lower lobe of the left lung and passed backward, making a wound in the left side of the heart an inch and a half in length and three-fourths of an inch wide and one-eighth of an inch deep. The ball had become lodged on the right side of the spinal column in the middle of the dorsal region, between the seventh and eighth ribs. The hole in the left side of the head was one-half of an inch in diameter, situated above the temple. The skull was fractured where the ball was embedded.

Dr. Stewart further testified that he recovered both of the balls from the body and presented them to the coroner. Either one of the shots in Warner's body would have caused almost instant death. The doctor's opinion was that that there could not have been a second wound inflicted by Warner after either of the shots. He stated that it seemed almost impossible for Warner to have self-inflicted the wounds on the left side of the body. He stated that in his opinion that had the wound in the head been made by his own hand, the gun would have dropped on the opposite side from where it was found. (*the gun was found on Roy's right side*)

Dr. Winger, who was present at the autopsy and took notes, stated that the range of both bullets fired into Warner was practically the same. The bullet in the head would have stopped all bodily functions at once. The bullet which tore away a portion of the heart would have produced death, but not so quickly as the wound in the head. He was at a loss to figure out how the man could possibly have inflicted both wounds upon himself.

The autopsy was finished, and Roy's brother from Brookville, John Warner, was allowed to take possession of the body and arranged its transfer to Brookville. The body of Roy arrived in Brookville on Tuesday morning, and a service was held from his parents' house in West Brookville. Burial then took place in the Brookville Cemetery.

The jury met again Tuesday afternoon and proceeded to the hospital to question Anna Peeler a second time. The only major change in her testimony was that she denied the story she had previously told about a lover in Buffalo and the letter she had supposedly written, and which Roy discovered. She said this was a fake story, even though she was the one who previously told this tale. She then said she was out with another girl in the company of two men, and this is why she and Roy fought. She said the men were just friends. She again admitted handling the revolver after the shooting but could not explain why she did it. The jury then adjourned until Friday morning. Anna Peeler was discharged from the hospital on Thursday and immediately taken to the Bradford City jail to await a verdict from the inquest, pending charges.

On Friday, the jury convened once again and heard from several acquaintances of the couple, who added little to the story. The main witness was Dr. James Walker. Dr. Walker testified that in his opinion, the injuries to Warner could not have been inflicted under the circumstances alleged by Ms. Peeler. He further stated that the wound on Anna's forehead was from a shot that was directed upward and outward, and the shot in the breast was directed downward. He speculated that by an easy movement of the wrist, Ms. Peeler could have pointed the gun upward and pulled the trigger, then reversing it, she could have shot downward toward the breast. Both wounds were superficial wounds. Dr. Walker was the physician that was called to the Mooney rooming house immediately after the shooting, and it was he who dressed Ms. Peeler's wounds. He said Peeler had told him Warner shot her then shot himself.

The jury then retired and soon came back with the decision that "Roy Warner came to his death between the hours of 4 pm and 5 pm on Sunday, the 2nd day of August, A. D. 1906 at the house in the rear of number 23 Davis Street, in the City of Bradford, County of McKean, State of Pennsylvania, by gunshot wounds in the heart and through the head, fired from a revolver in the hands of some person unknown to this jury."

District Attorney Mayo, while recognizing that the verdict was noncommittal as to who did the shooting, stated that he was confident that there was enough evidence to show that Ms. Peeler was the shooter and had indeed murdered Mr. Warner. Mayo made out first-degree murder charges against Peeler, and a warrant was issued to Ms. Peeler at the Bradford jail charging her with the murder of Warner. Peeler, denying any involvement in the murder, was taken before Judge Williams and committed to the McKean County jail in Smethport, pending a grand jury hearing on the charges.

While Peeler was in the McKean County Prison, the public at large in Bradford were divided as to whether she was innocent or guilty of the charges. An editorial, something that would be prejudicial today, brought out the prosecution's points in great detail. How Roy was able to shoot himself twice in fatal locations with his left hand when he was right-handed was the main question. Why did Warner not make sure Anna was deceased before shooting himself? It was shown that it would have been impossible for Roy to shoot Anna the way she described and more impossible for him to shoot himself with his left hand while lying prone on the bed. Why did Anna pick up the pistol and place a spent shell in the chamber right after the shooting? Many thought this was not the actions of a grieving lover. Also, it was noted that Roy had already been moving his possessions out of the room that very day and had rented another room. As Roy was the main breadwinner, Anna would have no choice but to move home with her father as she would not be able to afford to live on her own without a job, something she did not have. All of these questions swirled around the gossip mills of

Bradford. Citizens were also under the opinion that even though Peeler might be convicted, she would be given the benefit of the doubt and receive a very light sentence, if any.

As Anna remained in the McKean County Prison, the judge appointed W. E. Burdick and Harry Wick as defense counsel. The grand jury met on October 7th and 8th, and after hearing the same evidence that had been brought in front of the coroner's inquest, they brought in a true bill in the murder charge of Anna Peeler in the death of Roy Warner. Bail was denied to Anna, and her trial was put on the December docket.

The trial of Anna Peeler for the murder of Roy Warner commenced on December 16th with the selection of a jury. It took an entire day, but in the end, H. E. Lundquist, Hamlin township, Frank Tupper, Prentisvale, Frank Potter, Kane, August Kraft, Kane, Edward G. Nelson, Ludlow, H. H. Williams, Rixford, E. A. Guenter, Corryville, J. H. Stull, East Smethport, Charles E. Johnson, Smethport, J. F. Eberspacher, East Smethport, J. R. Foote, Smethport and Peter Olson of Keating Township formed the jury.

Anna was represented by three attorneys, W. E. Burdick, Harry Wick, and John Mullin. District Attorney Mayo represented the Commonwealth. Judge Bouton presided.

Mayo made the prosecution's opening statement in which he proposed to show that Roy Warner came to his death from pistol shots fired by Anna Peeler. Coroner Sherman was the first witness called, and he described the scene at 23 Davis Street in Bradford when he arrived. He found Warner dead with two gunshot wounds, one to the head and one to the chest. The pistol lying on the bed beside Warner's right side. Ms. Peeler was seated in a chair near Warner's body but was not excited but pale. He relayed what Peeler had told him about the shooting.

Dr. J. B. Stewart, who performed the autopsy, was called. He believed that the wound in the breast was a fatal one. He also described the wound in the head as also just as fatal. He said both wounds had powder burns, showing they had been fired at close range. Upon cross-examination, Dr. Stewart did say Warner could have fired the shot into his head if he inflicted the shot in his heart first.

Dr. J. W. Walker also testified. Walker stated that both wounds were fatal, and if the wound in the heart was inflicted first, the victim might live for a very short time. He told of the course of the bullets that had produced the superficial wounds on Ms. Peeler, these being in an upward manner to her temple and in the left breast downward and outward. Upon cross-examination, Dr. Walker stated that it would not have been possible for Warner to shoot himself in the heart after firing into his brain, as all motor functions would have ceased with the shot in the brain.

Attorney Burdick countered Dr. Walker and asked him if he ever heard of the famous crowbar case, wherein a man had been engaged in blasting, and a bar of iron had passed through his head and he afterward lived. The doctor said he was not familiar with the case.

Dr. Warner was called next and provided a detailed description of the crime scene. Blanche Meyers testified as to her observations as well. Chief M. D. Murray of the Bradford Police described the scene in detail also and described how Anna had told him about the letter she had written to a man in Buffalo. When Roy had discovered the letter, this had been what caused the argument. Several more witnesses testified as to what they observed that day, both prior to and after the shooting. Samuel Mooney, the landlord, identified the revolver as belonging to himself, and he testified that both Roy and Anna knew of its location, but he did not know how the weapon ended up in their possession.

The prosecution then rested, and the defense immediately called for a motion to acquit for their client, Anna Peeler. They cited the fact that there was only circumstantial evidence that Anna had been the one who pulled the trigger and there was no direct evidence through admissions or a third party. Judge Bouton took the argument into consideration with a decision being made the next morning. Court then was adjourned for the evening.

The court was called into session on December 18th at 9 in the morning. Judge Bouton said that he had made a decision, and then he instructed the jury to find a verdict of not guilty because the prosecution failed to provide any evidence that Ms. Peeler had indeed murdered Roy Warner.

Anna Peeler, much relieved and comforted by her family and friends, left the courthouse a free woman after having been jailed since the week of the death of Warner. Anna traveled back to Lewis Run to live with her father, and the Warner family traveled back to Brookville, sure that justice was not served.

Although there was strong circumstantial evidence pointing to Anna as being the shooter, it was not beyond a reasonable doubt. Modern-day forensics would have solved this case, one way or the other. In researching this case, I tended to consider Anna guilty, but also would not have convicted her as she never admitted anything. Everything did point to her, however in a case I researched in Johnsonburg, and which I will be writing about in *Volume IV of Elk County Murders*, the same type of injuries to a man, but with two shots to the head was ruled a suicide. How is that possible, you ask? You will have to read to find out.

Warner's grave in Brookville.

Double-Crossed

Tallini's grave at St. Bonaventure Cemetery in Allegany.

John Barber (*brother of Joe*) was one of the most brutal and feared chiefs of the bootlegging syndicate in Olean, New York. The power he possessed reached as far away as Buffalo and Johnsonburg, and he was a man who could make anyone disappear without a trace. The members of the Olean and Bradford gangs knew never to cross him or his directives. Barber acted without fear of law enforcement as he was widely believed to have bought off the police and judiciary. He reportedly could have his underlings released from criminal charges with a simple phone call to the authorities. When Barber was gunned down on an Olean street in broad daylight in May of 1925, a power vacuum immediately developed. Stepping into this vacuum was Vincenzo Tallini (*alias Jimmy Firpo*), who was known as a close associate and underboss of Barber. Tallini chose Dominic Pisano as his underboss, and they began to consolidate the power that Barber had previously wielded. Tallini and Pisano were just as cold-blooded and ruthless as Barber was, and they quickly eliminated what little resistance they encountered. It should be noted that Joe Barber, the brother and close confidant of John, had already fled Olean and moved to Bradford. The new Olean crime duo began to demand respect and alms from the former Barber territories and were miffed when they found they were receiving resistance from the Bradford operations. Tallini and Pisano discussed this resistance and decided that they must eliminate this threat to their authority. Several of their sources in Bradford and Olean had told them who was interfering in their consolidation of power, and they made plans to neutralize this threat. Through their sources, they were informed that their target would be most vulnerable in the early morning hours of July 31st, 1925, when he would be leaving his house unprotected to volunteer at an Italian fundraising breakfast scheduled for that morning. Tallini and Pisano used this intelligence to formulate a plan to eliminate the last and most serious obstacle to their total control of the Barber empire. They recruited two of the intelligence sources as their hitmen and made final plans to travel to Bradford on that Thursday night to complete their first major hit.

On Thursday night, July 30th, Tallini set out from his residence in his new Nash sedan. He was observed picking up his cohort Pisano at an Italian market on North Union Street at around 8 pm and then picked up the two "hitmen" at an unknown location. Tallini's sedan was spotted driving through Olean later that night with four occupants, and soon the sedan was headed towards Bradford. Later in the evening, an acquaintance observed the Tallini sedan in East Bradford, and they saw four occupants in the vehicle. The vehicle would not be seen again until the next morning, and this time, it contained only two deceased occupants. Tallini had earlier decided that their rival in Bradford must die a horrible death and armed one of his hitmen with a double-barreled sawed-off shotgun. When one is assassinated with a double-barreled sawed-off shotgun, the wound and indeed the damage to a body would be all that the community would talk about. Tallini was on a mission to not only kill his opponent, but he also wanted to send a notice to any other rival that if they interfered with his reign, they would suffer the most extreme death. Sometime after midnight, Tallini pulled into the Bradford Brewery parking lot, and his hitman guided him to a vacant storage shed behind the brewery to wait until the anointed time when they would make the hit. The men talked and joked about how this hit would allow them all to make the fortune that Barber had previously acquired. Tallini assured his "hitmen" that their future in his organization would be solidified by their service. At around 4 am, the time his source said they would find his target unprotected, Tallini began to put the key into his ignition. He would never finish this simple action.

As Tallini reached to put the key in the ignition, he felt an arm around his neck and heard a loud burst followed by intense pain in his left side; in his last moments of life, he realized that he had been double-crossed and would never live to see his wife or child again. Pisano was grabbed around the neck simultaneously and a bullet slammed into his head before he could react. The "hitmen" then pushed the passenger seat forward and exited the vehicle, and while doing so, Pisano's body shifted sideways, and his feet fell out of the sedan. The interior of the automobile was covered in blood and brain matter as the men escaped. The executioner of Tallini discarded the double-barreled sawed-off shotgun nearby. Both of the hitmen were never seen again or at least were never identified. The ultimate double-cross had taken place.

At around 7 in the morning, an employee of the H. C. Bemis Lumber Company was on his way to work when he noticed the Tallini sedan parked halfway into the brewery shed. He could see one occupant seated in the driver's seat and the second occupant's feet hanging out of the passenger side door. Not expecting this to be a murder scene, he figured these were two drunks sleeping off their hangovers. When he arrived at the lumber company a short time later, he mentioned what he witnessed to a coworker. His sighting intrigued his coworker, who thought he would have some fun with the "drunks," and he went to investigate. He never forgot what he encountered for the rest of his life, and he made the police promise never to reveal his identity, as he feared what happened to the duo would happen to him.

The scene that McKean County Detective Jack Allison, Bradford Police Chief Travis, and State Police Corporal Mullaney saw when they arrived must have been horrific. If you are aware of the damage both barrels of a sawed-off shotgun can do, you would understand why. This is part of the reason this type of weapon was banned in the United States because of the lethalness of this gun. The windows to the sedan were closed when the murder took place, which kept the brain matter and blood enclosed in Tallini and Pisano's tomb.

The murder car was a virtual blood bath. The side windows, dash, and windshield were covered with a film of blood and brain matter. Tallini's right arm was still stretched towards the ignition with the key held firmly in his hand. After taking pictures of the gruesome scene, the bodies were removed from the vehicle and searched. Looking at the license plate and viewing papers found on Tallini, the authorities realized the men were from Olean. Contact was made with Olean Chief of Police Dempsey, who knew the names of the victims. He headed to Bradford to formally identify the individuals, whom he had previously identified as having taken over the Barber "gang", when Barber was assassinated several months prior. Dempsey arrived before the bodies were removed and formally identified Vinzenzo Tallini and Dominic Pisano as the two murder victims. The sawed-off shotgun found nearby was the only clue left behind by the killers.

Bradford Police Officers Keenan and Fairbanks were called to bring the patrol wagon to transport the bodies to the Still Undertaking Rooms. The back compartment of the wagon was covered with sheeting to contain the blood and matter oozing from the bodies. Coroner H. Clay Heffner directed the removal and formed a coroner's inquest at the funeral parlor. Heffner appointed William Benedict, Webster Drew, D. H. Whiteman, V. M. Simons, O. A. Crandall, and John McCutcheon to the jury. Doctor's Joseph Kervin and S. H. Haines performed the autopsies. The doctors found that both barrels of the sawed-off shotgun had been unloaded in Tallini's right side, blowing a horrific hole in his right side that could not have been survived due to the damage done. They also found marks upon Tallini's neck, which indicated he had been forcibly held before the fatal double-barreled load. In Pisano's head, they found that an entire load of .38 caliber pistol rounds (*five total*) had been emptied into his head, even though the first round would have proved fatal. Finger marks were also observed upon his neck, indicating he was placed into a stranglehold before being shot. The pistol was not recovered at the crime scene. Both men were found to be carrying loaded .38 caliber pistols, but only Tallini had identification and $9 on his person. Pisano only carried a pistol. His identification was made by Olean Chief Dempsey. The jury ruled that both Tallini and Pisano came to their deaths by persons unknown to the jury, and the families of the victims were notified that they could come to Bradford to collect the bodies.

Early on Saturday morning, the Tallini and Pisano families sent representatives to Bradford, who transported the bodies to Olean. The double funeral for Tallini and Pisano took place from St. John's Catholic Church in Olean on Monday morning. The number of mourners reportedly rivaled those who attended John Barber's funeral which had fifty cars. The funeral procession proceeded along North Union and West State Streets and ended at St. Bonaventure's Cemetery. The procession was led by automobiles flying American and Italian flags, which were followed by an Italian band playing the funeral dirge. Following the band walked fifty men closely followed by three trucks carrying flower arrangements. The hearses carrying the two deceased men came next, shielded by an honor guard. Immediately following the hearse were Tallini's wife and small daughter and Pisano's family, who made up some of the fifty cars in the total procession. Intermingled in the procession was a number of undercover law enforcement officers looking to record who had attended and who had not in search of the elusive suspects. Unfortunately, the authorities were unsuccessful in identifying any viable suspects at the funeral, but truth be told, they were most certainly there.

The double-cross murders of Tallini and Pisano were never solved. The men had only been in control of the Olean syndicate for two months when they met their demise, and as one can see, they never really were in control. Soon a new boss took control, perhaps the one who had more control of the men John Barber left behind when he was assassinated. If forensic science was as advanced as it is today, the killers more than likely would have been identified. As it was, the investigation soon went cold, and another syndicate murder was the talk of the town.

The Nash sedan like Tallini drove.

A Friendly Game of Poker

St. Bernard's Cemetery where Gariciulo is buried.

Alcohol and a good old fashioned game of poker are never a good pairing. Tempers flare, and when you mix firearms into the situation, you have a recipe for disaster. One such "friendly" game of poker amongst countrymen took place in Lewis Run in 1916. By what few accounts that ever were released, the afternoon progressed quite joyously until some unforeseen and unexplained circumstance arose.

On the Sunday afternoon of October 8th, 1916, a group of Italians in Lewis Run had gathered at a local residence for a beer social. A game of poker was then begun, and all who were present drank beer freely and either participated in or observed the game. Two gentlemen, Frank Pisano and John Gariciulo began arguing, and their dispute disrupted the card game. They were asked to go outside and leave the rest of the party in peace. Pisano and Gariciulo stepped outside of the house, where they continued to argue. A gunshot was soon heard, and the men stopped playing the game and went outside to see what had happened. Lying on his stomach was John Gariciulo, who had an obvious bullet wound to his back. Frank Pisano stood over him with a pistol in his hand. Clem Cresci, described as a close friend of Gariciulo, did not even stop to ask any questions and shot Pisano point-blank in the head, just above his eye. Pisano crumbled to the ground while Cresci took off running. The rest of the party stood in amazement at the situation in front of them. Several men attended to Gariciulo, who was conscious, and carried him to his boarding house to provide first aid. Other men carried the unconscious Pisano to his boarding house. Word spread throughout the village of Lewis Run, and soon the streets were filled with onlookers. The quiet, sunny afternoon peace would soon be filled with activity, something unusual in this locale.

Bradford Police Chief Neal received a call at around 5 o'clock from a resident of Lewis Run, reporting a possible murder in that village. Bradford Police Captain Foster received a phone call from a relative in Lewis Run at about the same time, and both men met up at the police station. McKean County Detective Robinson soon joined them, and all three raced to Lewis Run in Robinson's touring car.

In Lewis Run, they found that both victims had been removed to their respective boarding rooms and split up to interview both of them while Captain Foster interviewed witnesses at the place of the shooting. Foster could find no-one who witnessed the shooting, and all of the men at the party were close-lipped and feigned not being able to speak English. Dr. R. A. Egbert of Custer City was summoned, and he examined both men and dressed their wounds. Egbert expressed that he believed neither man would survive their injuries. Pisano, who had regained consciousness, was interviewed in his bed and would not disclose any information. Gariciulo was also interviewed, and although he spoke fairly good English, he would not discuss what had led up to the shooting. The Koch ambulance arrived shortly, and both men were transported to the Bradford Hospital.

One Lewis Run resident told the officer that the man who shot Pisano had disappeared along the B. R. & P. Railway tracks in the direction of Howard Junction. The suspect in the shooting of Pisano was identified as Clem Cresci. An English-speaking Italian who knew Cresci volunteered to help the authorities search for him. The search party walked along the railway tracks and checked the undergrowth on both sides of the track the entire distance to Howard Junction without results. On the reverse search, about halfway between Lewis Run and Howard Junction, Cresci was spotted hiding in a clump of bushes. County Detective Robinson made the arrest and took Cresci to Lewis Run, where he was positively identified and subsequently removed to the Bradford jail.

At the Bradford Hospital, Dr. Egbert, who accompanied the injured men from Lewis Run, was joined by Dr. Wade Paton. The wounds were properly cleaned and bandaged, but the prognosis released to the press was that neither man was expected to survive the night. Both of the men refused to make any statements on what had happened, and the authorities had to rely on what little witness statements they had taken. The authorities charged Clem Cresci with attempted murder in the shooting of Pisano, and they awaited the outcome of surgery on Gariciulo to see if he survived. The bullet that had entered Gariciulo in the back had penetrated his intestines, and he was not expected to survive for very long.

Pisano, despite being shot above his right eye, made an amazing recovery from his wound. Pisano was released from the hospital within a week and was taken to the Smethport jail after a brief hearing in front of Justice Foley. He was held on an attempted murder charge, pending either the demise or recovery of his victim, Gariciulo.

Gariciulo lingered in and out of unconsciousness at the hospital for most of October and the beginning of November. An infection had set in, and he was reported to have been in great pain. Dr. Paton, his attending physician, kept the authorities apprised of his daily condition. Despite the best medical care that could be given during this time period, Gariciulo succumbed to his injuries on November 6th. Gariciulo was interviewed multiple times before his death but never told the authorities why Pisano had shot him. He did admit that Pisano was the shooter; he just would never explain what had happened, only that some "disagreement" had taken place, and he was shot as he attempted to leave the scene of the argument.

The remains of Gariciulo were taken to the Still Funeral Parlor, and services were held there on November 14th. Gariciulo, while having been in the United States for fourteen years, had no immediate family in the area, and his service was attended by a small number of friends from Lewis Run. He was forty-five years of age when he met his demise and had been born in Italy. He passed on the address of his mother in Italy, and Coroner Sherman wrote a letter edged in black to her explaining the circumstances of her son's death. Gariciulo was buried in Saint Bernard's Cemetery after a brief Roman Catholic service.

Pisano was taken in front of Justice Foley on Wednesday, November 8th, in Bradford and given a preliminary hearing. He was charged with first-degree murder in the death of Gariciulo and plead "not guilty." He was returned to the McKean County jail to await his formal trial, where the penalty could be death. Pisano never said he did not shoot Gariciulo; he just would not explain the circumstances and why he had done so. Rumors spread throughout Lewis Run and McKean County that all of the men involved were members of the infamous "Black Hand," and this was the prevailing thought. As any seasoned investigator will tell you, there is usually some truth in all rumors, and one must follow the rumor to find the truth. Cresci, meanwhile, was also incarcerated in the Smethport jail, and he too would disclose no further details about the shooting.

Pisano, in consultation with his attorney, decided to plead guilty to the charge of second-degree murder, and thereby he avoided any chance of the death penalty. Judge Bouton sentenced Pisano to a term of twelve to twenty years in the Western Penitentiary. He showed no emotion as he was sentenced, and the scar above his eye was quite prominent when he was escorted from the courthouse. Cresci, on the other hand, claimed he shot Pisano in self-defense and chose a jury trial. After a relatively short trial, Cresci was found guilty of attempted murder of Pisano and was sentenced on the same day as Pisano to one to two years in the Western Penitentiary. Cresci was released in a year and eventually made his way to New Castle, where he died in 1956, never having revealed any details of what had transpired that day in Lewis Run. Pisano served out his twelve years and was also released.

Mistaken Identity

Colonel Parker's tomb located near where Roy Himes lost his life.

Hunting season was once a dangerous time of year to be in the woods. A million sportsmen entered the wilds of the Commonwealth in search of game, and people shot in mistake for wild game was much more prevalent than today. Prior to 1959, hunters were not required to pass a state-sponsored hunter safety course, and the use of fluorescent orange was not mandated. Once the state required all hunters in the Commonwealth to pass a hunter safety course, shooting incidents decreased by eighty percent, quite a success. With the introduction of mandatory wearing of fluorescent orange, the woods are much safer than in the past. The hunting season of 1951 was especially deadly in McKean County. Three people were shot and killed, either mistaken for wild game or by the careless handling of a firearm. Chester Deptule of Erie and only sixteen years of age, was shot with a .30-.30 rifle by one of his companions who had tripped, and Chester later died of his injuries. Ray Himes, a school principal from Romney, West Virginia, was killed by a man in mistake for a turkey, and Oliver Olson of Prentisvale also died as the result of a stray bullet fired by a hunter. The last two cases resulted in prosecutions due to the negligence of each act.

Roy Garland Himes, thirty-two, of Romney, West Virginia, had traveled to Parker Run at Gardeau in McKean County in search of the elusive wild bear. He was accompanied by Ray Michael also of Romney and Earl Poland of Shanks, West Virginia. The trio had occupied a cabin in nearby Keating Summit since Sunday, November 18th, and were hunting turkey and bear. Mr. Himes, a principal at an agricultural school in Romney, made the trek to McKean County each year as a much-needed break from his stressful job. The men shared beers and stories and generally enjoyed this time in the woods, far away from their wives and the stress of life. The men were skunked on the first day of bear season and looked forward to going out on Tuesday morning. Roy decided to switch to turkey hunting and packed his turkey call into his red vest.

The men went out early that Tuesday to their usual spot, a mile and a half in the back of Parker Hollow. Roy began using a turkey call, and two turkeys answered. As Himes aimed his rifle in the direction of where the turkeys were, the morning silence was shattered by the sound of a high-powered rifle. Roy never knew what hit him and immediately collapsed and died within seconds. Mr. James Irwin of Washington, PA, was around one hundred and twenty yards away from Himes. He heard the turkey call and the turkeys answering and saw a patch of red in the bushes. He fired his .30-.30 rifle at the object. Irwin walked up to where he shot and immediately found the now deceased body of Himes. Irwin yelled for help, and soon other hunters gathered around Himes' body. They could see that Himes was dead, and they decided to put together a litter to carry the body to the road, a mile and a half from the location. When the men reached the road, they loaded Himes' body into a jeep and traveled to Keating Summit, where they called the game commission and the state police.

State Policeman William Vath of the Kane substation answered the call and was joined by Game Protector William Shirey. They interviewed Irwin, who never denied he had done the shooting and who readily cooperated with the investigation. The body was moved to the Gallup Funeral Home in Port Allegany, where an inquest was held by Coroner Elmer Beatty. Dr. F. E. Guenther performed the autopsy and found that the bullet had entered the left arm of Himes and traveled through the main aorta of the heart, cutting it in two. Both lungs were also seriously damaged, and several ribs were broken. Death was instantaneous. Game Protector Shirey stated he examined the scene of the shooting and said the area was covered with four to five inches of snow with no brush covering. The coroner's jury brought in the verdict that Roy Garland Himes came to his death as the result of a gunshot wound fired by James D. Irwin, stating that in their opinion, death was due to negligence in that Mr. Irwin did not use sufficient precautions before shooting. The jury was composed of C. F. Boller, S. S. Cray, Charles Catlin, Ralph E. Johnson, Earl Sykes, and S. D. Krepps. Irwin was taken before Justice of the Peace Arnold Field, where he pled guilty to the charges and was jailed at the county lockup on a $1,000 bond. He was soon released on bond. Irwin expressed much regret at his actions. He was scheduled for the December term of criminal court.

The body of Himes was prepared for burial at the Gallup Funeral Home and shipped to Romney, West Virginia, for burial. Himes was survived by his wife.

The case against Irwin was moved to the spring 1952 term of the court where Irwin pled nolo contendere (*no contest*) to a charge of killing a human being in mistake for game. Judge Hubbard accepted the plea and sentenced Irwin to a suspended two to five-year prison term. The sentence was suspended on the condition that Irwin paid $1,000 to representatives of the deceased and also placed him on five years of probation. Irwin's hunting license was also suspended for five years. For the rest of Irwin's life, he regretted his careless actions.

Cady Hollow where Oliver Olson lost his life.

On Thanksgiving day in 1951, Oliver Olson of Prentisvale planned to take his nephew, Paul Stromberg of Wrights, Pa, turkey hunting in his favorite haunt of Cady Hollow. They arrived at the hollow shortly before daybreak and walked to their stand where they sat and waited until daylight arrived. Olson and his fifteen-year-old nephew enjoyed their times hunting together and whispered back and forth. Oliver had spotted turkeys throughout the hunting season in this hollow and told Paul they had a good chance of seeing one. The hunters were sitting with their backs against a tree and watching the hollow below. At around 9:30 am, a shot rang out nearby, and Oliver let out a gasp and slumped over. Paul reached over to rouse his uncle and found that he was unconscious, with blood flowing from a wound on his right side. Paul began to yell for help, and soon several men approached from behind.

George Kucenic was hunting near where Oliver and his nephew were sitting. He saw a turkey and fired his .35 Remington at the bird and missed. As he walked towards where the bird landed, he heard another shot that sounded very near, and this scared him. Kucenic ran up a small ridge and found his hunting partner, Edward Baughman. Almost as soon as he met Baughman, they both heard screams for help directly below them. They both ran towards the shouting and found a very agitated Stromberg pointing to the body of his uncle. Both men could see that Olson was deceased and tried to calm Stromberg down. The boy said he did not know what to do, and neither did the men. The boy was feeling the body and seemed sure there were no signs of life. Paul kept crying, "let's get him out of here; let's get him out of here!" The men carried the body down to the foot of the hill, a distance of about a mile. The boy was sent ahead to find the road. The men came to the road, and a pickup truck approached.

The body was put into the bed of the truck, and they all rode down the valley until they reached Kucenic's truck. They transferred the body to his truck and drove to the Gallup Funeral Home in Port Allegany. Game Protector Cecil Hancock and McKean County Detective Merle Dickinson soon arrived, and a coroner's jury was formed by Coroner Elmer Beatty. The jury found that Mr. Olson had come to his death from "a gunshot wound fired by an unknown person." The bullet was extracted and later found to have been from a .35 caliber rifle. Hancock had questioned both Kucenic and Baughman at the first meeting in the funeral home and had elicited from Kucenic that he was carrying a .35 caliber weapon that day. At the time of the questioning, Hancock did not know that this was the caliber of the shell that had killed Olson.

Olson was forty-six years old when he died on that cold mountain. He was married to Jeanette Olson and lived in Prentisvale, which is close to Rixford. Oliver was employed as a carpenter at Bovaird and Seyfang in Bradford. His funeral service was held from the Emanuel Lutheran Church in Bradford, and his remains were interred in the McKean Memorial Park.

Kucenic traveled back to his home in Westmoreland County shortly after the incident without admitting to anything. After it was discovered that the bullet that killed Olson was from a .35 caliber weapon, Detective Dickinson reached out to Westmoreland Game

Protector Jack Logan to go and collect the weapon from Kucenic and question him regarding the matter. During the questioning of Kucenic, he admitted that he had fired a shot that day, and it may have resulted in the death of Olson. Kucenic stated: "On November 22nd, at about 10 am, our hunting party consisting of myself, Edward Baughman and William Craig were hunting in Cady Hollow, Liberty Township, McKean County, Pa. We were tracking a bear which I had missed the night before. I was walking along, trying to find the bear tracks. I stopped and glanced to my right, and a huge bird came flying low. I shot at the bird – it seemed to falter a little – and went into the laurel. I made three or four steps forward. Then a shot rang out. It felt as though it were near me. Being a little frightened, I ran up a hill. When I got almost to the top, I saw my friend, Mr. Baughman, at the same moment we heard a cry for help. It seemed to come from the front and left of me. Mr. Baughman and I immediately ran in that direction to investigate. When we reached this point, we saw a young boy. We later discovered his name was Stromberg, and he was fifteen years old. He was the one who called for help. When we reached him, he was at a distance of about one hundred yards from where I fired at the bird. We saw a body. The boy was frantic. He immediately said he didn't know what to do, and neither did we. The boy had been feeling the body and seemed sure the man was dead – there were no signs of life. The young lad couldn't seem to make up his mind what to do or what he wanted us to do. He kept crying, 'Let's get him out of here – let's get him out of here.' Mr. Baughman and I carried the body down to the foot of the mountain, a distance of about a mile. As we approached the foot of the mountain, we told the boy to go ahead of us and try to find a road. As we came to the road, a pickup truck approached from the top of the mountain. The driver of this truck assisted us in transferring the body and the boy further down the valley, at which point we transferred the body from this truck to my truck and headed into Port Allegany. We took the body to the Gallup Funeral Home."

The statement given to the game protectors was transmitted to Detective Dickinson, who conversed with the game commission and filed charges against Kucenic. Kucenic was charged with shooting a human being in mistake for game, which could carry a sentence of two to five years in jail and an assessment of damages from $500 to $1000 payable to the estate of the victim. Ten-year revocation of one's hunting license was also a penalty. Kucenic was also charged with failure to render assistance after a hunting accident and failure to report a hunting accident to the game commission. Kucenic's rifle and shells fired from the weapon were sent to the state police laboratory for testing to see if they matched the bullet removed from Olson. Kucenic returned to McKean County and was arraigned before Justice of the Peace Gavin McCoy of Port Allegany on the charges. He posted bail and returned to Westmoreland County. Kucenic pled not guilty and demanded a jury trial.

The trial of George Kucenic commenced on Monday, June 2nd, 1952, in the Smethport Courthouse. Kucenic was assisted by Attorneys Robert Apple and James Isherwood. Assistant District Attorney Guy Mayo represented the Commonwealth. Judge Charles Hubbard presided. The trial took five days, and many witnesses were called. The most significant information provided at the trial was from the state police ballistic experts, who testified that the bullet removed from Olson had been fired from the weapon owned by Kucenic. The jury retired on Friday afternoon and took twenty hours to reach a verdict. Judge Hubbard stated that this was the longest deliberation of a jury that he had ever seen. The jury was sequestered in the courthouse throughout Friday night and finally signaled they had reached a verdict on Saturday morning. The verdict was "not guilty," but with the stipulation that Kucenic paid all court costs associated with the case. Judge Hubbard released Kucenic with the stipulation that he pay the bill that would be provided post haste. Kucenic returned to Westmoreland County and never returned to McKean County. He paid the court costs and lived the rest of his life in his hometown. He died in 2002, still believing that he did not fire the fatal round.

The Inheritance

The location of the Wagoner farm today comprises the University of Pittsburgh's Kessel Athletic Complex.

A strong motive for murder is inheritance. When one perceives they will not be getting what they believe they deserve, there often is a plan to eliminate what stands in the way. People have committed all types of crimes to gain and protect what they see as their property. One such case happened in the old Bradford of the 1890s. I am not sure justice was served in this case, but it is a very interesting case indeed.

Calvin Hancock was a retired laborer who moved from address to address in the city of Bradford. He had lived in Bradford for thirteen years, but rarely at the same location. His life changed for the best in 1892. Calvin was walking the streets of Bradford when he met the widow Wagner. Mrs. Wagner was afflicted with cancer but still had a lot of spirit in her. She was carrying several parcels, and Hancock offered to carry them to her residence. Mrs. Wagner took Hancock up on his offer and thus began a relationship that would end in tragedy and the loss of Hancock's freedom. Mrs. Wagner owned considerable acreage about a mile outside of Bradford on Washington Street, directly across from the Hebrew Cemetery. The farm boasted one hundred and twenty acres upon which twenty oil wells were leased to a local oil concern. Mrs. Wagner was rumored to be worth $25,000, quite a fortune in 1892. The farm also had a large house with multiple bedrooms on both floors. Hancock eyed this property as a place he could finally set up roots and quickly became a good friend and confidant of the aged Mrs. Wagner. Mrs. Wagner had previously entered into an arrangement with Mr. George Hutchinson in which she would provide room and board in exchange for labor on the farm. She also entered into this arrangement with Hancock, and he quickly moved in and made himself at home.

Mrs. Wagner was seventy-one years of age and had seven children, four boys, and three girls. Her husband had died several years prior, and she had since developed terminal cancer. Three of her daughters and two of her sons lived in Bradford. Her son Frank lived close to the farmhouse and was not happy that Hancock had moved in. Frank spoke with several of his siblings, and they all agreed that Hancock was overstepping his boundaries. Frank had regularly visited his mother, and Hancock was heard telling him to leave as he was not welcome. As Mrs. Wagner became sicker with cancer, she was mostly bedridden and could not intervene in these verbal arguments. Hancock began to raise additional livestock on the property and procured a considerable amount of chickens. One night someone visited the farm and stole every chicken that Hancock had. Hancock also raised hogs, and several times in the fall, a hog turned up missing. Hancock suspected it was Frank and threatened him. Frank also began to follow Hancock on his walks to town, and several times he noticed Frank trailing him. Hancock confided in his daughters what was happening, and they implored him to leave the Wagner farm, but he refused. The tense situation reached a climax when one night in early December, dynamite was exploded next to the Wagner farmhouse. Hancock believed the dynamite was meant to scare him into leaving the Wagner farm. Hancock, instead of being scared away, went to Constable Spreeter and swore out charges accusing Frank of having been the culprit. Spreeter did file charges against Frank, and he was awaiting a hearing when he met his final jury.

On the night of December 15th, 1892, the feud came to a head. Frank Wagner had returned to his house after his Friday work shift, and like many, he drank several glasses of whiskey to celebrate the end of a hard work week. He was joined by his sister Isabel, and as he drank, they both discussed Hancock and how they despised the man. Both had attempted to get Hancock to leave their mother's house. They feared Hancock was planning to marry the old widow and thereby cut them from their inheritance. Frank's sister, Isabel, mentioned that she wanted him to go up to the old homestead and get certain gas fixtures and pipes for her house. Frank and Isabel went to their mother's house, and when they found the doors locked, they knocked loudly. Hancock said they needed to go away and leave him and their mother in peace. Frank then went to the back door of the house and broke his way in. Frank insisted on taking the gas fixtures and ignored Hancock, who was making threats and attempting to bar Frank from leaving with the fixtures. The loud argument soon turned physical, with Frank pushing old Hancock out of his way. Hancock retired and returned with a revolver and shot at Frank several times. The first two shots missed Frank, but the third hit him in the left side. Frank, realizing he was mortally wounded, ran into a back apartment of the house and fell forward upon the floor dead.

The news of the shooting spread quickly through the neighborhood, and in a short time, a crowd gathered at the Wagner farm. Officer McGraw and Coroner Slocum were notified about the shooting and arrived at the farm at about 2 am. They found several of Frank's sisters crying hysterically, with Frank's wife cradling his body in the back room. After examining the remains of the deceased, the coroner permitted those who were present to remove the remains to the residence of the deceased, which were a short distance from where the tragedy occurred.

Coroner Slocum empaneled a jury on Saturday morning to investigate the killing. Fred Matteson, John Wilson, W. W. Cheney, C. S. Morrison, Thomas Connelly, and P. J. Crowley were chosen. The jury went to the Wagner homestead to examine the scene of the shooting, and they then viewed the remains. They began to take testimony.

Hancock testified that Frank had been at the homestead twice before the deadly shooting. When Frank left the second time, Hancock had locked the outer door and retired to Mrs. Wagner's bedroom. He heard Frank break down the outer door and come into the dining room. He told Frank to leave and held the door to Mrs. Wagner's room shut with his body when Frank attempted to enter. He said he was joined by Mrs. Wagner. When Frank had left the second time, he said Mrs. Wagner had told him there would be trouble, and she gave him her deceased husband's pistol to protect them. As Mrs. Wagner and himself held the door, Mrs. Wagner begged her son to leave. "The door finally gave in, and Frank rushed in and hit me with a blow to the eye. I think he hit me with his fist first and then with something else in his hand. He grabbed me by the collar and threatened my life. He then struck me in the breast. I pulled the revolver and fired at him. The shot did not hit him, for he still held my coat. I fired again, and he then let me go and ran into the other room and then into the storeroom where he fell dead."

Mrs. Wagner was unable to go to the city hall because of her condition, and she gave her testimony to the jury while they were in the house. She said that her son Frank had come to her house at half-past ten on Friday night. She said she was deaf and could not distinguish the conversation between Frank and Mr. Hancock, but she knew they were quarreling. She said Frank and her daughter Isabel had stayed until midnight then left. Mr. Hancock had come into her bedroom to warm himself by the fire when she heard voices outside. She got up to look and saw Frank and five others working on the gas pipes. She told Frank to come back in the daylight and Frank said he had no time in the daylight and was doing this now. She said she thought he might be doing more dynamiting and was very frightened. She said she pleaded with them to all go away, and they refused. Frank then came to the back door of the kitchen and broke the lock to gain entrance. She and Mr. Hancock then closed her bedroom door and braced themselves against it to bar Frank from entry, pleading with Frank to leave. After Frank broke down her bedroom door, she retreated upstairs and saw nothing more until Frank was dead. She said she knew her son was drinking.

The jury then retired to the council chambers, where they continued to hear testimony. George Hutchinson, the only eyewitness to the shooting, testified next. He said he lived at Mr. Wagner's house and heard the trouble, which made him get out of his bed. He said he had just taken a seat at the dining room table when he saw Hancock open the door to Mrs. Wagner's bedroom and fire a pistol at Frank. "Frank ran out to the backroom, and I followed him. I said, Frank, are you hurt? Frank fell, and I tried to lift him, but he fell back down and was dead. He did not speak after being shot. Wagner was about three feet from Hancock when he was shot and standing still with his arms at his sides."

Isabella Raymond, sister of the deceased, then testified. She said she went with her brother and James McGarvey to the homestead at midnight to get some gas piping. She did not know what provoked the shooting and only heard Hancock tell Frank if he did not leave the house, he would shoot.

The jury then went to Frank's residence, where Doctors Gibson and Johnston performed a postmortem on the deceased. The bullet that killed Frank struck him in the left arm on the outside, halfway between the shoulder and elbow into the back of the base of the elbow and into the chest, breaking the third rib. It continued on and penetrated the upper lobe of the left lung, severing the artery above the heart and lodging in the right lung. Death was within seconds.

The coroner's jury, after deliberating, rendered the following verdict: "That Frank Wagner came to his death between the hours of 1 am and 3 am on the morning of December 10th, by a pistol shot fired from the hand of Calvin Hancock, at the Wagner homestead, in Bradford Township."

Coroner Slocum then went before Alderman Barlow and swore out a warrant for Hancock's arrest on a charge of murder. On Saturday evening, Hancock was brought before Alderman Barlow and waived a hearing. He was taken back to the Bradford jail to await transport to Smethport in the morning. Hancock's daughter, Mrs. Lew Gowdy, visited her father in the Bradford jail on Saturday, and she and her two sisters were much distressed at these turns of events. An application to admit Hancock to bail was submitted to McKean County Judge Morrison; this was unsuccessful.

Frank Wagner was around forty years of age and employed as a carpenter at a novelty works company in Bradford. He was married and had several children. He had been arrested on a complaint filed by Hancock regarding the dynamiting that had recently occurred on the Wagner farm, and the case was to have been brought into court the following week. Frank was on bail when he met his demise. Friends and acquaintances of Wagner said he was an industrious and hard worker who was also most generous with his time and willing to help those in trouble or need. His one fault lay in his tippling alcohol, but all said he was no drunkard. Frank was buried in the Wagner Family Cemetery located on Washington Street.

The trial of Calvin Hancock began on February 27th in the Smethport Courthouse. J. M. McClure represented Hancock, and the Commonwealth was represented by District Attorney Bouton, who was assisted by Attorney Eugene Mullin. Judge Morrison presided. The jury was composed of L. J. Gallup, W. Brayton, Michael Miller, John Karnes, John Paul, W. I. Oviatt, Fred Falkenburg, O. S. Evans, E. A. Barden, John Brown, G. Dudley, and W. B. Smith.

The prosecution's case rested on contradicting the testimony of Hancock at the coroner's jury. Mrs. Frank Wagner testified that a day or two before the shooting, when she and her husband were passing the Wagner homestead, Hancock had said to them, "I will shoot the whole Goddamn mob of you." She also testified that she never knew of any trouble between her husband and Hancock until he had taken up residence with her mother in law. She said her husband was not intoxicated the night he was killed.

Mrs. Diana Storey, another sister of Frank's, testified that she had lived in the homestead up to a month or two before the murder. She was helping care for her mother, who had terminal cancer. She said at that time, Hancock lived in an outbuilding on the farm. When she moved out around Halloween, she returned every day to dress her mother's cancer. She said when she returned late one night; she had found Hancock had taken over her bed and was now sleeping in the main house. Hancock made it unpleasant every day she visited. She heard Hancock say, "those Wagners have no business here", which was directed at her and her siblings. She also heard Hancock say, "if one of the Goddamn Arabs come here tonight, I will shoot them", and also say if they came during the daytime, they shall knock like anyone else. Hancock also told her and her son that "I am not afraid of you; I can lick any two of you. I will have every one of you in the penitentiary." She never heard her brother threaten Hancock that night or any previous night.

Mrs. Isabella Raymond, another of Frank's sisters, then testified. She said it was at her request that Frank and others went to the homestead to collect the unused gas pipe that night. She had previously had the pipe laid to an outbuilding, and when she moved, she wanted the pipe retrieved and laid at her new residence. She said they went that night as Frank said he had to work the next day, and this was the only time he could collect the pipe for her. She said after Frank had taken up the pipe, she went into the house to tell her mother that they had collected the pipe and had not disturbed the line running to her house. She was in her mother's bedroom, where Frank and Hancock were arguing about the pending court case regarding the dynamiting incident. She heard Hancock say to Frank, "you get out of here, or I will shoot you!" She says Hancock had a revolver. Her mother said, "Do go away; I don't want any trouble here." She asked her brother to go, then Hancock accosted her and said, "you get out of here too, you goddamned bitch, or I will shoot you!" Both she and Frank headed into the kitchen, and Frank stopped to gather his lantern. Isabella continued outside when she heard the shots. She ran back in and confronted Hancock. "You have not shot Frank, have you?" and Hancock said, "Yes, goddammed you, and I ought to shoot you" he then put the revolver in my face and shoved me away. I ran down to the road and met up with Hancock again as he was fleeing the scene. He took hold of me again; she said she struck him and broke free.

John Goodrich, a nephew of Frank, next testified that he assisted his uncle that night collecting the pipe. He said they had only picked up the unused pipe and had not disturbed any of the gas piping to the main house. Goodrich said after they had collected the pipe, Frank told them to take it down to the road, and he would go in and tell his mother that they had not disturbed any other pipe. While waiting at the road; he heard three pistol shots in rapid succession. He started up the road towards the house and met Hancock fleeing the house. Hancock had a revolver and said, "Get out of my way, or I will kill every one of you." Goodrich said he hid under a hitching post for four or five minutes. He then headed towards his home and saw Hancock once again having a tussle with his aunt, Mrs. Raymond. Hancock had a lantern and revolver on him, and in the tussle, the lantern was broken. Hancock headed back towards the homestead and said, "I dare anyone to follow me!"

James McCready and Ed Caldwell of L. Emery & Company Store next testified that Hancock had purchased a revolver in their store a few days before the shooting. Hancock had said he would "shoot to kill the bastards," meaning the Wagners. He also said he needed the pistol to protect himself as the Wagners had been exploding dynamite about his place.

George Hutchinson, the only eyewitness to the shooting, was called next. He said he was sleeping on that Friday night when Hancock had awakened him and said there would be trouble. He said he was sitting at the dining room table, three feet from Frank. He said Frank was standing with his arms at his side, and Hancock opened the door to Mrs. Wagner's bedroom, looked at himself and Frank, then drew back reached out with a revolver and fired three shots. Frank turned and went out through the kitchen and into the storeroom where he fell. He followed Frank and found he was deceased and then saw Hancock threatening Mrs. Raymond. Under cross-examination, Hutchison said that Frank had come into the house three times that night. After Frank had left the first time, Hancock and Mrs. Wagner were hunting for the revolver and asked him if he had seen it. After the coroner and several police officials testified as to their involvement, the prosecution rested.

The defense then opened their case by calling Mr. Hancock to the stand. Hancock testified about the trouble he had had with the Wagner children. Frank had made many threats to him and said he would kill him (*Hancock*) if he did not leave his mother's house. He said he was seventy-four years old and a farmer by occupation. He said he had taken up residence at the Wagner farm in April under an agreement with Mrs. Wagner. He said he had stayed in an outbuilding until November when explosions of dynamite had shattered the glass in the outbuilding's windows, and it was too cold to continue living in there. He then moved into the main house and slept on a lounge in Mrs. Wagner's bedroom. He said there were seven different dynamite explosions which he felt were all aimed at himself in an attempt to get him to leave the farm. He said he swore out a warrant to have Frank

Wagner arrested for these acts, which was in the process when the shooting occurred.

The night of the shooting, Hancock said that Frank had come to the house with a subpoena for his mother to come to Smethport to testify in the upcoming trial. Frank talked to his mother and then accused Hancock of dynamiting the house. Frank then came up to him and shook his fist and swore he was going to kill him. Frank left and, after a while came back saying he was going to take some gas piping. Hancock then noticed men and women about the house and then he awakened Hutchinson and looked for his revolver, thinking trouble was brewing. He told Mrs. Wagner of the people about the house and she locked the doors and she yelled out the door to Frank and told him to go away and not come into the house again. Frank broke into the back door, and he and Mrs. Wagner both held the door to her bedroom shut as Frank was attempting to gain entrance to her bedroom. Mrs. Wagner then told him to shoot through the door. Hancock said he fired low down through the door to scare Frank. Frank burst open the door, which caught Hancock's foot and ripped his nail loose. Frank then reached into the room and hit him under the eye, then struck him on the cheek. He said Frank swore he would kill him and that he (*Hancock*) would never leave the house alive. Frank then grabbed him by the breast and tried to pull him through the opening of the door, swearing he would kill him. Hancock told Frank to let him go, and Frank said he wouldn't, so Hancock shot at Frank again, and he let go this time. Hancock then said he heard Mrs. Wagner arguing with Mrs. Raymond and heard her say, "Oh, don't you hurt me!" He heard Mrs. Raymond tell her mother, "Frank is shot, and you told Hancock to do it!" He then said he grabbed a lantern and started out of the house and met up with three people who knocked the lantern out of his hand. He ran in a different direction and ended up in Bradford, where he turned himself in to Constable Spreeter.

Mrs. Eliza Wagner was then called to the stand. She testified as to the employment of Hancock and his coming to her house to live. She said on the night of the shooting, her son had come in around 11 o'clock, and he and Hancock had some words about going to Smethport the following Monday regarding the dynamiting charges. Eliza said she was hard of hearing, so did not hear what was said but could tell by their actions that it was confrontational. She said she told her son not to have any trouble. My son asked about taking the gas pipe. He then went out to get the pipe. He came back into the house with a lantern, and she did not hear what was said. She admitted that she was scared because of the previous episode with the dynamite. She said she looked out the door and saw six people and begged them not to explode anything. She said she locked her bedroom door, and someone came and pounded on it. She assumed it was Frank. She held the door closed when Frank was kicking it, and she said, "please don't. Oh Lord!" She did not hear the shots or see the shooting and went into another room to escape. She said she did not give Hancock her husband's revolver and did not tell Hancock to shoot.

Dr. Chadwick was called, and he testified that he examined Hancock at the jail when he was first brought in. He found a bruise on this cheek, a black eye, a scratched hand, and his breast was injured. He also thought one of Hancock's ribs was cracked. Several character witnesses were then called who described Hancock as an industrious individual who never drank nor partook of tobacco. They all said Hancock had an impeccable reputation. The defense then rested.

The prosecution in rebuttal then brought into court the door that hung between the sitting and dining room of the Wagner house. They showed that there was only one bullet hole in the door and that there were no other signs of a struggle or abrasions suggesting the door was kicked and broken in to.

The prosecution then presented their closing arguments and highlighted the fact that Hancock's story was full of contradictions. Mullin said that Mr. Hutchinson, the only witness to the fracas, had not seen Frank force open the mother's bedroom door but had seen

Hancock reach out and shoot while Frank had stood with his arms at his side. Mullin called for a guilty verdict of first-degree murder.

The defense presented that Hancock was severely threatened the night of the shooting by Frank. With the history of bad blood between the men and the prior dynamiting incident, Hancock was justified in his shooting of Frank for his safety. Hancock was justified in protecting himself and should be acquitted.

The jury was out for twelve hours when they returned with a verdict of "guilty" to the charge of voluntary manslaughter. Judge Morrison had the option of sentencing Hancock to one to ten years of incarceration for the guilty verdict, and by his own reasoning, he chose the maximum penalty. Hancock was sentenced to a term of ten years in the Western Penitentiary and fined $500, quite a hefty sentence. The jury had to choose between first-degree murder, second-degree murder, voluntary manslaughter, or acquittal. Public opinion was that Frank was not guilty of murder and that the jury chose voluntary manslaughter because it was the lowest charge besides acquittal they could come up with. The judge apparently believed Hancock was guilty of second-degree murder as the sentence he imposed was within those guidelines. Many thought that ten years was a life sentence for this seventy-four-year-old man, and he would never survive. Public sympathy was with Hancock when he was led away to the Western Penitentiary, thought never to be seen again as a free man.

Mrs. Eliza Wagner died at her home on the Wagner farm on February 7th, 1895, from cancer. Her surviving children were at her side when she took her final breath. She was seventy-four years old and had been a resident of Bradford for fifty years. She came to the area in 1844 with her husband from Pultney, Steuben County, New York, and settled in Bradford Township. At the time of her arrival, there were but three houses where Bradford now stands. She was survived by three sons, John of Salamanca, Arthur of Frecks Mills, Albert of Bradford, three daughters, Diantha Storey, Isabella Raymond, and Della

Goodrich, who all resided in Bradford. She was buried next to her husband and her son in the Wagner Family Cemetery.

Calvin Hancock served his sentence in the Western Penitentiary in Pittsburgh, and he was largely forgotten, with most assuming he had passed away while in prison. The *Bradford Era*, however, ran a story on February 12th, 1901 that the venerable citizen of the county who long had been a prisoner, had been released and relocated to the city of Bradford, having been released early due to good conduct. Hancock had survived the unsurvivable. The article also mentioned that Hancock had shot and killed Frank Wagner in self-defense, something that was not decided in the original court case, but something that still must have been on the minds of his admirers. Hancock lived for a while with one of his daughters and was last reported to have become a ward of the city and living in the city infirmary in May of 1902. He was described as having his mentality and spending his days reading with his only handicap being his deafness. Hancock was never mentioned again in the news, and it can be surmised that he passed sometime shortly after this last report.

The Assyrian Peddlers

The spring where Tomas & Shibley stopped for a drink. The abandoned cabin was located somewhere behind the spring.

Many different nationalities make up the American population. One particular group were descendants of an ancient empire known as Assyria. The Assyrians became stateless centuries ago and were a minority discriminated against in the lands of present-day Syria and Iraq. The remaining Assyrians in that area today still suffer. The few that were let into this country in the late 19th century tended to continue their established profession of traveling from town to town and peddling goods and services. This profession grew out of their nomadic life in the middle east.

Two Assyrians, Ellis Tomas, and Kenen Shibley, came to the United States in the 1890s. The men traveled the railways, peddling wares, tools and clothes. They often spent nights in desolate locales and slept out under the stars when no shelter could be found. Tomas and

Shibley had eventually traveled to North Western Pennsylvania and regularly traveled the rails from Punxsutawney to Olean. In Olean the men would replenish their stock and head back along their route to Punxsutawney. In Punxsutawney they would begin their trip again, headed back towards Olean. On one of these trips, one of the partners would meet up with foul play in a situation clouded with inconsistencies and mystery.

Tomas and Shibley had left Punxsutawney around the end of June of 1898 and began their route to New York. The duo reached Saint Marys on July 21st and spent several days there. From Saint Marys they traveled to Glen Hazel and then Straight Creek. After leaving Straight, the pair were walking along the train tracks in the direction of Clermont when they stopped at a small spring to quench their thirsts. Two other men also stopped to get a drink. While the men were drinking, a powerful thunderstorm with driving rainstorms hit the area. An abandoned lumber camp was situated directly up the hill behind the spring and all of the men soon were inside and out of the rain. Four went into the shanty but only three would emerge alive.

Ellis Tomas was fleeing for his life when he came upon the house of the Buffalo and St. Marys Railroad section foreman's house which was located along the train tracks outside of Clermont. Tomas knocked loudly upon the front door and asked for help. C. M. Rhodes, the foreman, answered the door to find the slight figure of Tomas standing impatiently on the porch. Tomas informed Rhodes that his companion, Kenen Shibley, had been killed in the storm a few miles back on the line. Tomas said his friend had been struck by lightning. Upon further questioning by Rhodes, Tomas changed his story and said it really was not lightning, but a tree had fallen on his companion. Tomas gathered up several of his men and told them to bring their axes as they would be removing a fallen tree. The men then followed Tomas the several miles to the shanty, which was located in close proximity to the railroad tracks. As the men neared the shanty, Tomas changed his story again to say that his companion had not been killed by a falling tree but at the hands of two "Americans."

The men reached the shanty and went inside. They found the body of Shibley lying on the floor; blood pooled around him. The deceased man had three gunshot wounds to the body, two in the back, and one in the neck. Rhodes decided the best thing to do was to leave the scene and body as they had found it and to notify the authorities. He and his men escorted Tomas back to Clermont, where he was turned over to Constable John L. Smith. Smith arrested Tomas and, on the search of his person, found he had $42, a knife, and a pair of scissors. Constable Smith escorted Tomas to the county jail in Smethport, and along the way, Tomas told him another story. Tomas said that he and Sibley had been invited into the shanty by two Americans. While inside, an argument arose over a mouth organ that Tomas had, and Shibley had threatened to shoot one of the strangers. One of the strangers instead shot Shibley three times from behind. Tomas said he escaped the shooting by jumping out of a window and running along the train tracks.

Rhodes gathered up the Sergeant Township authorities and led them to the cabin. They transported the body to Clermont, where it was examined by Dr. Burg Chadwick and Dr. Rutherford. They found three shots had entered Shibley's body. One had passed through his neck, while the other two penetrated his heart. Death would have occurred shortly after the shots had entered the heart. They also found that Shibley had extensive bruising and cuts about his head and face, but none would have proved fatal. The dead man's front pockets were turned inside out when found and two satchels were laying next to his body that appeared to have been rifled through.

McKean County Coroner Sherman traveled to Clermont and impaneled an inquest over the body of Shibley. Members of the jury included: Bart Olson, foreman, T. H. Ryan, L. Bayer, Patrick Gaynoy, E. J. Slides and E. Martin.

Ellis Tomas was sworn first. He said that the dead man was a countryman, and they had been peddling their wares along the railroad. They started their journey in Punxsutawney, then to Houtzdale, Clearfield, Penfield, Clairton Mines, Shawmut Mines, Centerville, and Saint Marys. They were in Saint Marys on Thursday night (*July 21st*). The duo then went to Glen Hazel, then to Straight Creek and from there to Cherry Camp, peddling all the way. Saturday night, they stayed at a railroad builders camp and left there around 8 am on Sunday morning. This camp was about fourteen miles from Clermont. They stopped for lunch at Matt Tolga's camp along the railroad and left there around one in the afternoon and stopped at a spring around three miles from the camp. They met two strangers at the spring, and then it began to rain. They all went into an abandoned lumber camp to get out of the rain. While they were in the camp, Shibley took out a mouth organ that he was peddling, and one of the strangers took the organ and began playing while the other stranger danced. The men asked the price of the organ, and Shibley said .25 cents. The man said way too much and offered .3 cents. The man started to walk away when Shibley grabbed him and said, "you pay me .25 cents, or I will shoot you." The second man then stepped up behind Shibley and shot him. "I heard three shots, and when the shooting began, I ran and jumped out the window. One of the men followed me and shot at me while I was running down the railroad track but missed. I then found the foreman's house and told him what happened."

C. M. Rhodes was called next. He lived at Wildwood, nine miles south of Clermont. He said that on that Sunday, he saw two peddlers going along the railroad tracks towards Clermont at about 10:45 am. The men said they had just come from Matt Tolga's camp. I went home and saw no more of them until around ten minutes to seven in the evening. Tomas knocked at my door, and when I opened it, he seemed quite scared and excited with perspiration running down his face. Tomas told him the storm had been quite violent and had killed his "butt" at the next camp. Rhodes asked Tomas if lightning had killed his "butt," and he said yes. He said a tree had been struck by lightning and had killed his butt. I called my men and told them to get the saw and axes and put them on the handcar. Tomas then said there was no tree on the track. When we arrived at the camp, Tomas was asked to show where his friend's body was. Tomas entered the camp first. I followed in and found Shibley lying on the floor with his back towards the door. I stepped over him and found a mark on his right cheek, under the eye, and blood on the forehead. I then said to him, Tomas, "lightning killed your butt?" He said, "oh no, two American men killed my butt." He said the American men killed my butt over a little bill, and over the settlement of this bill for the mouth organ, the shooting occurred. Afterward, he said a man with a blue suit did the shooting. When brought to Clermont and questioned on this point Sunday night, he said that he meant his "butt" had on a blue suit. We then proceeded to Clermont, and when I discovered that the murder had been committed in McKean County, I turned this over to the authorities. We left the body and packs at the old camp that night. We did not see any indication of a struggle in the camp.

J. F. Keating was sworn next. He stated he was the foreman of the coal mines at Clermont and that he first heard of the murder on Sunday night around 8 o'clock. Keating said he went to Smethport to notify the district attorney and sheriff and returned home that same night. He went with the authorities to the lumber shanty on Monday morning and observed the body of Shibley. Two opened packages were next to the body, and an old passbook with Arabic writing was also discovered. Keating went through the dead man's pockets which appeared already to have searched and only found .22 cents. He said Shibley did not have a gun on him, and his pants pockets were turned inside out. A .22 bullet was sticking out of the cabin wall directly in front of where Shibley had fallen.

Constable John Smith testified that he resided in Clermont and had taken Tomas into custody. When he searched Tomas, he found $42, a knife, and a pair of scissors, but no pistol. He said he questioned

Tomas about what had happened, and Tomas told roughly the same story as he did on the stand.

Tomas was recalled to the stand. He said after the shooting, he had jumped out of the window and ran up the railroad grade to escape. He said Shibley had around $20 to $25 on his person. He also said they had been peddling together for about six months.

Joe Bogdlge, an Assyrian merchant from Olean, next testified. He stated that he had known the deceased for around nine months and had supplied him with merchandise for his peddling operation. He said the deceased still owed him $1.34 on his accounts. He also said he had known Tomas for about a year and a half and had also known that Tomas and Shibley worked together and seemed to have a good relationship. Shibley wanted to form a partnership with Bogdlge in Olean and told Bogdlge that he had $1,500 in a bank with which to form a partnership.

Several other individuals testified to roughly the same stories and statements that Tomas had made when reporting the murder. The inquest adjourned to discuss the evidence and returned with the following verdict: "That Kenen Shibley came to his death by gunshot wounds fired by some person to them unknown." The jury also concluded that sufficient evidence had been produced to justify the holding of Ellis Tomas for trial at the next term of criminal court. Justice Stefahauer made out the necessary papers, and Deputy Sheriff Clarke brought Ellis Tomas to Smethport and lodged him in jail to await a formal trial.

Kenen Shibley was described as a man of slight build, five feet six inches tall, swarthy complexion, black eyes and hair, high cheekbones, and a retreating chin. After the autopsy his body was wrapped in a blanket and placed in a simple wooden coffin. A local priest provided a Christian service, and his remains were buried in an unknown location somewhere near Clermont, far away from the middle eastern town where he was born.

Ellis Tomas, the accused murderer, was described as being about thirty years old. He stood five feet, seven inches tall, and was solidly built. Tomas had dark hair and eyes, a dark complexion, and had a black mustache with prominent features. Public opinion was almost totally against Tomas, and commentaries in the newspapers of that time blatantly said he would probably be the next person to be hung in McKean County. Tomas never uttered any admission of guilt throughout his arrest and imprisonment and was described as a model prisoner while awaiting trial for the murder of Shibley.

The trial of Ellis Tomas commenced in Smethport on Tuesday, December 13th, 1898. District Attorney Gorton assisted by Attorney Eugene Mullin, represented the Commonwealth. Attorney P. R Cotter of Eldred represented the defense. Judge T. A. Morrison presided. After some drama, a jury was selected that included John B. Pierson, Tomas Crawford, C. M. Boardman, T. B. White, C. A. Ross, P. Gallagher, Z. S. Brunner, A. H. Wilcox, J. F. Bonvaird, John Hughes, James Landergran, and M. S. Geary.

The prosecution focused on the several variations that Tomas had told regarding the murder of Shibley. It was purely a circumstantial case, but the penalty they were seeking was the death sentence for Tomas.

C. M. Rhodes, section foreman for the Buffalo & Saint Marys Railroad, was the first witness for the prosecution. He reiterated his account of how Tomas said at first lightning had struck his friend, then how it was a tree that killed his friend, and finally how it was an American that killed his friend. Rhodes added that Tomas told him the American had worn a blue suit and later said that the victim was the one in the blue suit.

Dr. Burg Chadwick testified about the autopsy he performed on the remains of Shibley. He found three shots in Shibley's body, with two entering the heart. The bullets were fired from behind, and either of these shots would have caused instantaneous death.

F. C. Livermore of Clermont testified that he had questioned Tomas about the murder and had been informed that four stout men had done the killing. Several more witnesses testified that Tomas had told conflicting stories of what had happened, but all said Tomas never admitted any part in the shooting. The prosecution then rested.

The defense began with an impassioned statement of the righteousness of their case and how only circumstantial evidence, and weak evidence at that, was presented by the Commonwealth. Cotter then called Ellis Tomas to the stand. Tomas appeared relaxed and thoroughly stuck to his story that Shibley was killed by an American, and the argument was over the price of a mouth organ that Shibley was peddling. Tomas contradicted the different versions of the killing that he had told, but continuously denied he had any part in the killing. The defense then called several character witnesses for Tomas and rested their case.

After an hour adjournment for lunch, Judge Morrison took control of the trial. The judge told the jury that there was not sufficient evidence in the case to warrant conviction of murder in the first-degree. If the defendant was guilty, he was guilty of murder in the first-degree, as he made no excuse for the alleged crime, but denied he was involved. If the death of Shibley was a murder at all, it was murder in the first-degree. The actions of the defendant at the time of the murder were very much unlike those of a guilty man, and he had explained in a very satisfactory manner how the murder occurred. The judge said that he felt justified in asking the jury to return a verdict of "not guilty." District Attorney Gorton and Eugen Mullin, attorneys for the Commonwealth, approved of the action of the court and also asked that a verdict of not guilty be returned.

The jury deliberated for a short period and returned with a "not guilty" verdict. There reportedly was much rejoicing from Tomas's friends who had gathered in the courthouse for the hearing. Tomas was released directly from the courthouse to freedom. Tomas reportedly continued to peddle his wares up and down the railroad for some time after the killing and then headed for parts unknown. The "murderer" of Shibley was never apprehended, and even though the district attorney agreed with the court that all they had was circumstantial evidence against Tomas, he still felt they had the right man on trial in the killing.

Pig Island

An old picture of Pig Island.

In the old Bradford, there was an "infamous" area known as "Pig Island." This area was really not an island but because of the depraved and immoral activities that took place within this section of Bradford, it was described as such. The locale certainly earned its reputation by housing the area's most sinful establishments where you could find anything of a depraved manner if you were inclined to walk on the wild side. Pig Island was located in a square of land that lay between present day Mechanic Street, Charlotte Avenue, Walker Avenue and East Washington Street. The main thoroughfare through this lustful area was Globe Street. Globe Street figures prominently in the police reports and newspapers of the 1880s and what a wild and fun time a night out on Globe Street must have been. Amid these establishments stood a non-descript saloon owned by Franklin "Frankie" Meadows. This saloon, as many similar establishments, had many violent and robustious incidents over the years, fueled by the alcohol they served. News accounts in the early 1880s had mentioned this particular establishment as having numerous incidents where the police were involved. Luckily, no deaths had taken place in this establishment until a loud and well-known rabble-rouser decided to make one of his infamous scenes at the Meadow's Saloon on July 1st of 1884.

The Meadow's Saloon on Globe Street was quiet for a Tuesday morning. Three men came into the bar at around 11 am and loudly ordered a beer from the proprietress, Frankie Meadows. Meadows, who was feeding her young daughter behind the bar, left her seat to serve the men. The "leader" of the trio, Jack Head, began to curse Ms. Meadows with foul language that even the press at that time would not print. Head called Meadows a whore and a piece of crap and demanded she serve all three on her knees. Meadows told the men to behave themselves, or she would make them leave. Head jumped up on the bar and grabbed Meadows by the hair and punched her, meanwhile saying he would kill her. Meadows told Head she did not want any problems with him and reached behind the bar to grab a revolver she had secreted there for just an occasion.

Head made an immediate exit out the front door of the tavern, and Meadows laid the weapon upon the bar. Head's companion then punched Meadows upon the side of her head. Meadows sat down to cry, and the large man said he was sorry; he did not mean to hit her. Her daughter began to cry, and Meadows picked the child up to console her. While rocking the toddler, Head returned to the bar and began to curse Meadows once again, saying he would not be bluffed by the handgun this time. Head jumped back upon the bar and walked on his knees to where Meadows rocked her baby. Head again grabbed Meadows by her hair, and Meadows yelled for all three men to leave the bar at once. Head's companions told him to leave Meadows alone and that they were going to leave. Meadows once again grabbed her weapon, and almost immediately, Head ran for the door. Meadows asked the other men to leave and to take Head far away from her saloon. The men said they wanted nothing further to do with Head and that Head had already gotten them into half a dozen fights earlier that morning.

Head returned to the bar for the third and final time and once again began cursing Meadows. He jumped up on the bar again and swung his legs over the bar in one quick motion, saying he was not afraid of Meadows, and he would take his revenge on her. Meadows told Head to leave her alone, or he would be sorry, but Head reached out to grab her once again. Meadows reached around with her right hand and secured her pistol. As Head went to punch her, she fired one shot at Head. A look of shock came over Head's face, and he looked up at her and quickly jumped down from the bar and exited the saloon. The men with Head exclaimed that if she was going to shoot blanks, she might as well shoot at them also, followed by raucous laughter.

Head left the saloon and collapsed onto Globe Street. A crowd was now gathering around his body, and the police were sent for. The police entered the saloon and secured the pistol after asking Ms. Meadows who had done the shooting. Meadows was arrested on suspicion of homicide and taken to the Bradford jail to await the findings of a coroner's jury. The body of Head was picked up and taken to the Webster Undertaking Establishment for an autopsy.

Frankie Meadows was arrested immediately after the shooting and lodged in the Bradford jail while Doctors Murdoch and Buss made a post-mortem examination of the body. They found that the bullet had entered at the fifth rib, about four inches below the left arm, passed through the right auricle of the heart, then through the lungs. The bullet then passed through the third rib, and finally lodged in the muscles just below the right arm. The doctors also found a significant amount of blood in the lower portion of the heart and believed that death would have been within thirty seconds after the fatal bullet entered Head's body.

On Wednesday, July 2nd, 1884, McKean County Coroner Dempsey empaneled an inquest into the death of Head. The men appointed to the jury included W. Graham, foreman, L. L. Clough, Lewis Powers, G. H. Hunt, Charles Bailey, and A. H. Weaver. District Attorney

McSweeney traveled from Smethport via the morning train and was the presiding officer of the jury.

Frankie Meadows was conducted from her cell in the City prison to the select council chambers for her examination. Meadows, described as a real beauty, also appeared to have been a fashionable dresser. She was described as wearing a black silk dress rather loosely fitted about the waist and trimmed in wide lace and bounces. She carried a little leather handkerchief bag on her arm, something that was described as the fashion of the day. She also wore a black alpine hat, trimmed with a heavy black feather plume. Meadows testified that at around 11 am on the past Tuesday morning; Jack Head entered her established and commenced the tirade of abuse upon her. She also testified that she did not know these men or Jack Head personally and could not recall if she had ever seen them before. Meadows did say that a group of men had come into her bar about five weeks prior and abused her much the same way as the day in question, and she believes these were the same men. Meadows testified that after abusing her for the third time and grabbing her hair, she decided she was not going to accept Head's abuse anymore. She grabbed her revolver and fired at Head.

Bradford Police Chief McCrea then produced the revolver and handed it to District Attorney McSweeney. The weapon was described as being a dangerous looking .38 caliber self-cocker, one which might have been a cowboy's favorite weapon on the western frontier. McSweeney then questioned Meadows.

Q. "What did Jack say when you shot?"

A. "He didn't say anything after I fired that I heard. Before this, when I warned him to let me alone, he said: "What in hell will you do?" One of the two men, after I had shot and Jack ran out, laughed, and said: "Ho, that was a blank cartridge. I'll let you shoot at me that way all day.'"

Q. "What did you do with the revolver after this affair?"

A. "I gave it to Mr. Prescott. Mr. Milligan came in and asked who did the shooting. I told him I did, and he advised me to get the revolver out of the way, and so I gave it to the first man that came in afterward."

Q. "Have you seen Head that morning previous to his coming into your place?"

A. "When I went down to the bottling works that morning, Head followed after me and hollered: "What is it? Tell me what it is, and you can have it! and all such guys."

Meadows denied that she and Head had any previous incidents which would have caused her to have a grudge towards Head and said she only fired after he grabbed her by the hair, and she believed he was going to hurt her or her child.

McSweeney felt he had enough evidence with Meadow's admission that he did not need further testimony for the coroner's jury to make a decision. He called the doctors to testify to their autopsy findings and briefly called Meadow's roommate Kittie Lewis, who backed up Meadows's actions on that fateful day. McSweeney then told the jury that they should make a determination on whether or not Meadows caused the death of Jack Head and should be held on such charges.

After a short conversation amongst themselves, the jury rendered the verdict that Jack Head came to his death from a pistol shot at the hands of one Frankie Meadows. Chief McCrea then had Meadows arraigned before Justice Wheeler with the verdict of the coroner's jury, and Justice Wheeler ordered Meadows to be held on a charge of homicide. Meadows was transported to the McKean County jail in Smethport to await a future grand jury on the matter.

Jack Head had only recently been employed by the Rochester & Pittsburgh Railroad. He had previously been employed by the B. B. & K. Railway and often made trips to Buffalo with the train as a brakeman. Head had been off on the day of the shooting and had a reputation as a troublemaker whenever he traversed the saloons of Pig Island. Head's hometown was Liberty, Sullivan County, in New York. His parents were notified of his death but did not claim his body. His remains were held at the Webster Undertaking Home, and it was said that many people, mostly out of curiosity, came to view his body. Head was buried at the city's expense in Oak Hill Cemetery.

The trial of Frankie Meadows for the death of Jack Head took place in Smethport on October 10th, 1884. Attorneys Mullin and McClure represented Meadows while District Attorney McSweeney represented the Commonwealth. The prosecution only called three witnesses, and their case was described as meager at best. The premise of the prosecution was that the shooting was unnecessary and that the defendant could have escaped by backing up to the saloon wall and thereby avoided the confrontation. David Ford, one of the men who had accompanied Head into the bar, told his version of events and said that while Head was loud and boisterous the whole day, he had never intended to hurt anyone and that Meadows overreacted to his humor. When questioned further, Ford said Meadows could have easily backed up and away from Head and instead shot him. Mrs. Spear, another occupant of the saloon at the time of the shooting, said she witnessed the events of the shooting and said that Head never placed his hands upon Meadows. Attorney Mullin, on cross-examination, caught both Spear and Ford in seven different and distinct lies and succeeded in discrediting their testimony.

The defense called Kitty Lewis to the stand. Lewis, the roommate of Meadows and a witness to the shooting, testified almost verbatim to the story told by Meadows and said she felt that Head was bent on hurting Meadows. McSweeney tried to discredit Lewis by saying she only testified to what Meadows previously said because she was a personal friend and roommate of Meadows and, therefore, would lie for her. Frankie Meadows testified to what she had previously explained and said she feared for her life and had threatened Head that she would fire her revolver if he did not leave her alone.

McSweeney delivered the Commonwealth's closing argument to the jury and implored the jury to find Meadows guilty of murder. McSweeney said that Meadows could easily have avoided shooting Head and instead chose to shoot rather than avoid the confrontation altogether. Mullin then told the jury that Frankie Meadows had no choice but to shoot Head on that fateful day. Head had not once, not twice but three times confronted Meadows and placed his hands upon her and pulled her hair. Mullin said the shooting was justified and that Meadows deserved to go home with her baby.

Judge Olmstead then charged the jury with an impartial plea that the jury consider the case carefully and the jury retired to consider the verdict. Within forty minutes, the bells of the courthouse began to ring, signaling the jury had reached a verdict. The jury foreman handed the verdict to McKean County Prothonotary Brawley, who showed the verdict to the judge. Brawley then read the verdict in which the jury found Meadows "not guilty." The packed courtroom all stood up in unison and clapped their hands and stomped their feet. The judge was not amused and promptly ordered the arrest of a man names McCorkle who was fined $15 for contempt of court. The judge ordered everyone else to sit down and remain quiet. The judge then dismissed the jury and Meadows.

As it was late on a Saturday night, the last train to Bradford had already departed. Meadows was offered a local hotel room to wait for the next train home on Sunday morning. She chose to return to her cell to sleep for the night. Meadows said she preferred her well-kept cell where she had spent the last three months, to a hotel room where a vulgar populace would gaze and stare at her and bother her all night. Early the next morning, the warden escorted her to the train station where she was met by Kitty Lewis and her baby, and they all alighted onto the train at 9:20 and arrived in Bradford around noon. Meadows continued to operate her saloon for several years after this incident, and eventually, she disappeared from the records; whether she married or moved is unknown.

The Saga of Francis Godino

Francis Godino.

The La Mano Nero or "Black Hand" was a mysterious organization that existed in the Italian immigrant community in the early part of the 20th century. This organization originated in the Kingdom of Naples in the 1850s and was brought to this country in the late 1800s when large numbers of Italian immigrants settled here. A small minority of these immigrants formed their own criminal syndicates within their respective Italian communities and preyed upon their fellow immigrants. It is claimed that as many as ninety percent of immigrants were victims of these local organizations at some time in their lives. The Black Hand targeted poor immigrants as well as some of the most successful ones with no discrimination based upon means. A typical method of the Black Hand was the sending of a letter to the intended victim, threatening bodily harm. These letters contained threats to kidnap loved ones, to burn down their homes or businesses, or even death. The letter demanded an amount of money to be placed at a specific location by a specific date, often at a grave in a cemetery. If the demand was not met, the threat was usually carried out. Sometimes the threats were not carried out by a letter but instead given in person. The Italian community knew when these criminals were operating in their areas and were deathly afraid of becoming victims of their extortion. It was only in later years that they began to fight back, and the Black Hand was then replaced by a more organized syndicate called "La Cosa Nostra" or the present-day mafia.

In Corryville, there was a large lumber operation around the turn of the century, which employed many Italian immigrants. These immigrants came to the United States to pursue their American dream, and most who came had no family in the States. The men worked twelve-hour days and often sent money home to Italy to support their extended families. Also, operating in the McKean County area was a group of "Black Hand" extortionists. These men lived off of the labors of others and were feared by all of the immigrants. The Black Hand was notorious in Italy, and many of the workers already had experiences with these miscreants in the old country. The Black Handers used informants to notify them when payday took place and conveniently showed up to take whatever money they could swindle. In a rooming house in Corryville lived thirteen Italians who all worked as woodcutters. Word was sent to the Black Hand in Olean that some of these men had a considerable amount of money in their possession and were planning to send the money to Italy. On the night of March 26th, 1906, a group of four Black Handers went on a mission to Corryville to get this money for themselves.

At around 7:30 that evening, a group of boarders in Corryville were busy cooking supper when there was a knock at the door and four men appeared. All of the strangers were armed, and they at once announced that they were collecting money for a sick Italian, and they expected all of the boarders to contribute. They were offered beer and dinner, but the men said they were there for the money and not food. The boarders stated that they had spent their pay at Smethport that very day buying provisions, and none of them had any leftover money to contribute for this "sick" countrymen. Loud arguments then started, and one of the intruders pointed a pistol at the boarders and started to wildly shoot in the house. Only one of the boarders had a pistol, and he went to retrieve it while the strangers retreated. He fired out the door towards the fleeing men, but none of his bullets hit their mark. When the smoke cleared, twenty-eight-year-old Giuseppe Tiberri lay mortally wounded with a gunshot wound to the chest. Tiberri expired shortly after the shooting, and the boarders sent a man to Smethport to inform the authorities. McKean County Sheriff Mitchell formed a posse and sent word to all of the outlying areas to be on the lookout for the four suspects.

In Eldred, night watchman Chell Olmstead was employed by the tannery. He had been informed the previous night of the happenings in Corryville and was on the lookout for four men. At around 6 in the morning, he saw four men matching the descriptions of the suspects walking along the train tracks in the direction of Olean. He phoned Officer Ives of Eldred and told him he suspected these men were the wanted men from the previous night. Ives lost no time in loading his pistol and was soon on the scene. Ives was dressed in plain clothes, and both men walked along the tracks and overtook the suspects. The suspects did not know that Ives was a lawman. After passing the suspects, Ives turned around and pointed his pistol at the men, and announced they were under arrest. Three men raised their hands, and when the fourth man went to reach into his breast pocket, Ives pointed his loaded pistol at the man's head. The suspect then raised his hands. Olmstead then relieved each man of their pistol, gathering three .38

caliber and one .32 caliber handguns. The men were then escorted to the Eldred jail. Ives phoned Sheriff Mitchell with news of his arrests and also phoned the sheriff of Cattaraugus County. Cattaraugus Deputy Sheriff Steele soon appeared at the Eldred jail. Steele had suspected the men were from the Olean area after he was informed of the shooting in Corryville and stated he would know the men when they were captured. Steel identified the men as Olean Black Hand and said he had arrested the ringleader just that past Monday. Steele charged Godino with brandishing a knife and threatening to kill a man at that time. Steele identified the men as Francis Godino, Rocco Daqui, Salvator Caruso, and Fillipi Frisina.

Sheriff Mitchell and District Attorney Mayo traveled to Eldred and took custody of the four men. Possidio Tiberri, a cousin of the dead man, was also brought to Eldred. One by one, the suspects were brought into the room, and Possidio identified each man as the ones who had been at the boarding house and who had killed his cousin. The authorities thanked Ives, who had single-handedly captured the suspects, and transported the prisoners to Corryville, where Coroner Hall was forming an inquest. In Corryville, additional boarding house residents identified the suspects.

Coroner Hall appointed Asa Champlain, Peter Cooney, L. W. Howden, John Stull, J. T. Morrison, and Henry Backus to the jury. Dr. McCoy, who performed the autopsy on Tiberri, was the first witness called. Dr. McCoy said the bullet which killed Tiberri entered the left chest two inches below the collarbone, slightly to the left between the second and third ribs, cutting through two large pulmonary veins of the left lung, striking the backbone and being deflected upward to the right lung where it was found. The man died within a few minutes from loss of blood.

Possidio Tiberri, the cousin of the dead man, then testified. He witnessed the shooting and said the four men had entered their residence at around 7:30 on that Monday evening. Tiberri said he had seen one of the men before but did not know who he was and said the other three were strangers. He said the men were greeted in a friendly manner and were offered beer and supper. "We came not for a drink but money!" the leader had said, "We need money to help a man who is sick."

Tiberri said the residents explained to the intruders that they had little money to give as they had purchased supplies just that day in Smethport. The intruders insisted on cash and would accept no apologies. The leader then beckoned Giuseppe Tiberri, who was standing in a doorway, to come into the room where they were. Giuseppe refused to approach. The robbers then drew their pistols and said, "come give us your money, or we will kill you!" and almost immediately began to shoot. Tiberri said he had purchased a revolver just that day in Smethport for a man who had been recently robbed in Moody Hollow. He said he had fired back at the robbers as they fled but had not hit them. He then positively identified all four men in front of the court while the leader, Godino, muttered veiled threats at him.

Godino, who had a limited understanding of the English language, then stated he wanted to speak. He began telling the jury that he was only in Corryville that night to look for work. Godino was informed that anything he said might be used against him, and he then did not make any further statements.

Sheriff Mitchell then presented the four firearms taken from the suspects and identified each suspect by name and which pistol had been confiscated from each. The jury retired and returned with a verdict that Giuseppe Tiberri came to his death at the hands of one of the four men. The four prisoners were returned to the county jail to await a hearing in front of Justice Knapp, which was to be called after the official warrants were completed.

At the hearing before Justice Knapp, Possidio Tiberri once again described what he had seen and positively identified the defendants. Godino claimed he had no idea why and what he was being charged with, and District Attorney Mayo plainly explained the charges to him. Godino made crude remarks and glared at every spectator in the packed courtroom. Nine additional residents of the boarding house positively identified Godino and his associates as being the ones who had entered their residence and subsequently began shooting. Several said that Godino fired first and that the bullet Godino fired is the one which killed Tiberri. Several of these men stated that they had seen Godino and Rocco Daqui in the area before. Godino stared down each witness and challenged them stating they had guns in their house. Each witness denied they had weapons in their boarding house, except for two shotguns, which were not used, and the pistol which Possidio Tiberri had purchased that very day. All of the witnesses expressed fear of the prisoners and were worried they would be released and come after them for their testimony. Godino smiled broadly when each man said this and crossed a finger across his neck to sinuate what he would do to them.

Sheriff Mitchell then produced the weapons that officer Ives had taken from the prisoners and identified which ones were found on each suspect.

D. M. Sliceban, Reuben Prontiss, and Arden Hastrom were called, and each of them testified that they had encountered the defendants in the vicinity of Corryville on that Monday night.

Ambroggio Jinblizzi then testified positively that Godino was one of the three men who robbed him of $100 on March 18th. He said he was compelled to hand over the money at the end of a revolver. He said he only recognized Godino from the four prisoners and the other three were strangers.

Ginunino Antonio testified that on March 18th, he too had been held up by Godino at gunpoint. Antonio said Godino searched his body but that he had no money on him that day. Monenfri Eddio stated that he, too, was held up on the 18th by Godino at gunpoint.

The hearing then concluded, and charges of murder were bound over to the criminal court against all four men. Additional charges of robbery were also lodged against Godino due to the testimony of several of the witnesses. The prisoners were returned to the jail and denied bond, all charged with first-degree murder in which the penalty could be death by hanging.

Francis Godino and his partners spent their days in the Smethport jail awaiting their respective trials. Godino, however, showed he was not a model prisoner. On May 3rd, he pretended to have a seizure, and his fellow prisoners called the Turnkey Welsh. Welsh found Godino lying upon the floor. He picked him up and placed him on the cell bunk. Godino then attacked Welsh, who was a large man. Welsh soon had Godino under control and handcuffed him while summoning the jail doctor. The doctor could find nothing wrong with Godino and concluded that he was feigning a seizure. Later that same day, Godino tore up his shirt and made a rope out of it. He put one end around his neck and the other through a grated opening. He asked a fellow prisoner to pull on the rope and thereby end his life. The other prisoner refused and called Welsh back into the cell. Godino then wielded a chair and attempted to hit Welsh in the head, but he was unsuccessful. Godino was then placed in a cell by himself and watched more closely to prevent any further antics.

On June 6th, 1906, the grand jury met and found true bills on the charge of murder against Francis Godino, Rocco Daqui, Salvator Caruso, and Fillipi Frisina. District Attorney Mayo decided to try each defendant separately with the trial of Rocco Daqui being adjudicated first.

The trial of Daqui began that same day in the Smethport Courthouse. Fifteen witnesses who were in Corryville, many in the house when the shooting took place, identified Daqui as being a participant in the holdup but also identifying Godino as the one who shot Tiberri. All four defendants were at the first trial, and it was noted that Godino listened to each witness's testimony with much disdain. It was also noted that several who testified at the earlier hearing had since fled the country and returned to Italy in fear of their lives.

Rocco Daqui then testified on his own behalf. He told the court that he was innocent of the charges. Daqui said he and Caruso were on a train to Corryville to look for work and that Godino and Frisina were also on the train. He said he knew nothing about the scheme to rob the Italians at Corryville. He said after the train reached Corryville, Godino mentioned something about money. When Daqui protested about going with him to the shanty, Godino insisted that he and Caruso accompany them. He told how, when they entered the shack, Godino called Giuseppe Tiberri to him and asked for cash. Giuseppe said he had none to give. He then said he saw Godino pull the revolver from his pocket and shoot at Tiberri. He said he did not fire any rounds but that he was indeed armed. He said all four then made their escape and followed the train tracks back towards Olean, where they were apprehended near Eldred. He emphatically denied shooting Tiberri.

A surprise witness for the prosecution was then called. He was a private detective named Lasa from Pittsburgh. He had made arrangements to be placed in the Smethport jail on a false charge of forgery, occupying the cell adjacent to Daqui. He testified that he overheard Daqui tell a catholic priest who visited him that he (*Daqui*) was present when the shooting occurred at Corryville and that he and the other defendants participated willingly in the attempted robbery. The case then went to the jury after attempts by Defense Attorney Gallup to have the indictment quashed were overruled. The jury returned with a guilty verdict of second-degree murder, and Judge Bouton sentenced Daqui to fifteen years imprisonment in the Western Penitentiary. Godino's trial followed the sentencing of Daqui.

The Godino trial began on June 12th in Smethport with the selection of the jury. F. B. Grantier, Charles E. Hampton, W. H. Huston, William M. McAllister, Calvin DeYoung, A. B. Lucas, H. H. Adsitt, W. J. Morris, J. W. Anderson, E. B. Chapelle, John Oviatt, and Harry

Rhodes were chosen. Attorneys E. L. Keenan and Thomas H. Morrison handled the defense of Godino. District Attorney Guy Mayo was assisted by his son, Attorney E. R. Mayo, in the prosecution. Judge Bouton presided.

The prosecution called the same witnesses that they had called in the Daqui trial. The numerous Italians who were in the woodchopper's camp in Corryville the night of the shooting, testified as to Godino being the leader and the one who shot Tiberri. They all confirmed that Frank Godino and his three companions came to the house, knocked for admittance, and were invited into the house. Godino did the talking and asked for money from the residents for an imaginary sick fellow countryman. Godino, failing to collect any money, then called Tiberri, who was in the kitchen, to come out into the living area. Godino asked Tiberri for money, and when refused, Godino emphasized the demand for money by deliberately pulling a revolver from his pocket and shooting at Tiberri. At the first shot, Tiberri fell. There were two other shots, according to witnesses. All of the other residents were frightened by these shots and hid under a table or rushed upstairs to avoid the bullets. Possidio Tiberri, the cousin of the victim, did return fire, but his bullets went wild and did no injury. Godino listened to this testimony with a stoic posture and appeared to handle the case with a coolness, something peculiar for someone who was facing the gallows if he were to be convicted. The prosecution called the medical experts next, and they rounded out the case for the Commonwealth.

The defense then called Frank Godino to the stand. Godino said he had arrived in this country sixteen years prior and worked in lumber camps ever since. Godino admitted that he was in Corryville and at the boarding house but that he only shot in self-defense after Tiberri fired at him first. He said he knew where his bullets went, saying only two bullets were fired in the house, with one going into a wall and one going into the floor. He said the third bullet was fired outside. He said he did not know that Tiberri was dead until he heard about it at the coroner's inquest.

In rebuttal, the prosecution called D. Therminy, a barber from Bradford. Therminy said he often acted as an interpreter. He was sent to interview Godino at the Smethport jail in May by the prosecution to get Godino's version of events. He testified that Godino had admitted to him that he was a member of the "Black Hand" and that he had gone about and visited several camps in the interest of the organization. He said Godino had also told him that he robbed a certain Rosario Fabino of $225 near Rixford a short time before the shooting in Corryville. Therminy then said Godino told him he had killed Tiberri and did not care what became of him because of the murder. The Black Hand people had failed to come to his (*Godino*) aid in this trouble, and this made him angry. Godino revealed the secrets of the order and also named the Italian in Olean who was the head of the organization in that section of the country. Godino also told Therminy where workers for the order were located. All of this information was in the hands of the district attorney and was very damaging to Godino.

Attorney Keenan then presented the closing statement for the defense. He expounded upon the law and pointed out for the jury that to be convicted of first-degree murder; it must have been premeditated. Keenan said that as Godino and Tiberri were complete strangers, there is no way that Godino could have premeditated this murder. Also, Keenan said that as there was no evidence of robbery, there could be no conviction higher than second-degree murder. Keenan said that the Commonwealth's evidence of an attempt to rob was lacking.

District Attorney Mayo closed for the prosecution by saying Godino killed Tiberri in cold blood and that by bringing the revolver to the attempted shakedown at Corryville, he showed premeditation to murder, whether or not it was someone he knew.

Judge Bouton then gave his directions to the jury, and the jury retired to the anteroom. The jury was out for four hours when the bells of the courthouse began to ring at 10 pm, signaling they had reached a verdict. The jury was polled, and they unanimously agreed to a conviction of "murder in the first degree," thereby sending Godino to the gallows. Godino, formerly stoic, finally realized the full impact of the words uttered by the jurors, and in despair, he began to wail in his native language a declaration of violence against those that had testified against him. He wept bitterly as he was taken back to his cell.

Attorneys Keenan and Morrison argued before Judge Bouton on behalf of their client with reasons why a new trial should be granted. Their points being:

First: There was no evidence to warrant a verdict above the second-degree.

Second: There was no evidence of an attempt to rob.

Third: Godino simply went to take a collection for a sick Italian.

Fourth: All the men were equally guilty.

Fifth: There was no evidence of premeditation to commit a crime.

Sixth: Everything considered, Godino was not given a fair trial morally speaking, although legally the trial was fair.

Judge Bouton considered the arguments and, in a quick decision, delivered his report. In the case of the Commonwealth of Pennsylvania vs. Francis Godino, Rocco Daqui, Salvatore Caruso, and Fillipi Frisina.

In the Court of Oyer and Terminer of McKean County, June term, 1906.

"And now, to wit, June 15th, 1906, Godino, being brought into open court in the custody of the high sheriff of said county, and the rule to show cause why a new trial should not be granted, returnable at this time, together with the motion and reasons for a new trial having been fully and carefully considered, it is now ordered that the said rule to show cause be discharged and the said motion for new trial and reason thereafter, be overruled and dismissed and the said Francis Godino being in open court in custody as aforesaid, and it is demanded of him if he hath or knoweth anything of say wherefore the said Court of Oyer and Terminer should not proceed to judgment and sentence against him, he nothing further saith unless as he before had said. Whereupon all and singular, the premises aforesaid being seen and by the Judge of the said Court fully understood, it is considered, adjudged and sentenced by the said Court: That you, the said Francis Godino, be taken from this place to the jail of the County of McKean, from whence you came, and within the walls or yard of the said jail, be hanged by the neck, according to law, until you are dead and you are now committed to the custody of the High Sheriff of the said County of McKean for the purpose of having the sentence carried into the execution. By the Court, Joseph W. Bouton, Presiding Judge."

Godino had nothing to say when this decision was given. He appeared haggard and depressed but did not give away his emotions and was taken back to his cell by the sheriff. His attorneys filed a brief with the Pennsylvania Board of Pardons and Parole in a last-ditch attempt to spare the life of their client.

Godino spent his days in jail attempting to prove he was insane in the hopes he would be sent to the insane asylum and thereby escape justice. He set the mattress on fire in his cell, headbutted the bars in his jail cell in a suicide attempt and talked to himself as if he was seeing things. None of these antics was seriously considered insane. His attorneys went before the Pardon Board in November to argue his case but were unsuccessful in getting the sentence reduced to life in prison.

Sheriff Mitchell received the word in January that Governor Pennypacker had signed Godino's death warrant on January 9th and fixed the day for the execution on February 26th, between the hours of 10 am and 3 pm. Mitchell informed Godino of the governor's order and the date on which it would be carried out. Godino showed no emotion and appeared resigned to his fate. The sheriff placed Godino on a death watch to ensure he did not harm himself and escape justice. Mitchell began to make arrangements for the hanging and had to decide whether to use gallows like those used to hang Ralph Crossmire or to build an old-fashioned drop-trap scaffold.

As February 26th came, Godino was reportedly in good spirits and resigned to his impending death. Sheriff Mitchell had re-constructed the same gallows that hung Crossmire, and they were tested in preparation. The sun shone brightly in Smethport on that fateful day. Father Doyle of Clermont came to the prison in the morning and was joined by Father Dugan to provide religious services to Godino. Godino appeared to be in a good mood and joked to his guard that "you will have no one to watch tonight; you are out of a job." Sheriff Mitchell went to Godino's cell at 9:30 am and read the death warrant to him word for word. Only a chosen number of spectators were allowed to witness the hanging, but many had gathered outside of the courthouse out of curiosity. A wooden wall had been built to hide the act from the public. At 10 am, the sheriff led the procession to the gallows, followed by Fathers Dugan and Doyle carrying a crucifix. Alongside Godino walked two men, Turnkey Welsh and Patrolmen M. C. Bain of Bradford. Spectators outside of the fence heard Godino loudly uttering a prayer as he walked to the gallows. As Godino reached the gallows and his eyes fell upon them, he was suddenly overwhelmed by emotion. Tears gushed from his eyes, and his normally strong voice became broken and fervid. "Ora Pro Nobis!" (*pray for us*) Godino replied to Father Dugan as the priest uttered the litany for the dying. The expression on the doomed man's face was described as one which all who witnessed would never forget. Every eye of the witnesses was also observed to be moist, including the *Bradford Era* reporter. Sheriff Mitchell then asked the prisoner if he had anything to say, but at the moment, Godino was loudly answering the priest's invocations in English, saying, "Lord have mercy upon me; Christ have mercy upon me!" Welsh and Bain strapped Godino's legs and arms and fastened the buckles. Godino said, "Lord, into the hands, I commend my spirit," when the black hood was placed over his head. A witness, Mr. King, then slipped the noose over Godino's neck and motioned to Sheriff Mitchell that all was ready. Sheriff Mitchell released the wooden trigger, which was attached to two hundred and ninety-seven pounds of weight. "Lord have mercy on me!" came from the voice under the cap; "Lord have mercy…." and then there was a sharp click, a creaking of the gibbet and the heavyweight suddenly released. The weight fell with great momentum and pulled the rope taught while the body of Godino dropped like a sack of potatoes.

Godino's body swung and thrashed, and it was immediately apparent that his neck was broken in the fall. A few convulsive movements of tightening and relaxing muscles were evident before the body became still. The body was lowered to the ground, and the medical personnel present examined the body and declared Godino expired. Undertaker Sasse then entered with a black cloth-covered casket and removed the remains for burial.

Godino's body was taken to the St. Elizabeth Cemetery in Smethport and interred in an unmarked grave. Fathers Dugan and Doyle officiated at the gravesite. No other mourners attended. Giuseppe Tiberri was previously buried in the same cemetery. The other two prisoners, Caruso and Frisina, were sentenced to the same fifteen years that Daqui received and served their terms and were deported after their sentences.

Shortly before his death, Godino had an interview with an *Era* reporter. Godino said that he had come to the United States at fifteen years of age from Calabria, Italy. His father had died while he was very young. He had come to America with his mother through the financial help of a man whom she had known in Italy. She had married the man when they arrived in Ossining, New York, where his mother still resided. Godino was not yet twenty years old when he met his death. He had followed various kinds of work and had eventually drifted to Olean. He said he was only in Olean a short period before the incident at Corryville. When asked if he was guilty of the charge he was convicted of, Godino said he was not sure. Godino said his accomplices also shot and he was not sure if his bullet was the fatal one. He said that no relatives had come to visit him during his confinement but had received letters from them. A final letter from his mother had arrived a day before the hanging and Godino read it again and again, the night before he died.

The Brewer House

Yohe's grave at the Syphrit Church Cemetery in Reynoldsville.

John Alex Yohe was born in 1856 in Reynoldsville to Peter and Mary Ann Yohe. John was part of a large German family who operated a farm on the outskirts of town. John had dreams of making his own life in the world and continuously sought to escape the confines of his farm. John had been bartending at some local establishments and dreamed of traveling to another locale where the town and opportunities were more robust. In a local paper, he read about a position as the head bartender at the Brewer House in Mt. Jewett, an up and coming town with many more patrons than sleepy Reynoldsville. Yohe took the train to Mt. Jewett, and after meeting with Mr. Brewer, he was hired as the new bar manager with a handsome salary. Yohe was exhilarated and rushed back to Reynoldsville to tell his parents about his new job. With tears and good tidings, Yohe left his parents' farm and returned to Mt. Jewett with a determination that only a new opportunity can present. Yohe quickly settled into life in the bustling village and, in short order, gained many friends and acquaintances not only through bartending but also after-work activities. On one of his visits to a local dry goods store, he ran into John Thompson, who was the general foreman of construction for the railroad. Thompson, a regular customer of Yohe's at Brewer's, was challenging the men in the store to lift a barrel of flour in a certain way. Thompson lifted the drum with ease and gently placed it back on the ground with barely a groan. Several men attempted to lift the barrel the way Thompson did and failed. Yohe, a large strapping farm boy, watched the attempts with humor and walked over and picked up the barrel with one arm and let it back down just as quickly. The men and women in the store clapped and cheered him on, but old Thompson was not so amused. Little did Yohe know that a grudge was born of this simple act, one that would end his dreams and ambitions forever.

At around noon on July 24th, 1886, John Thompson entered the Brewer House bar and ordered a whiskey. It had been several weeks since the flour barrel incident, but Yohe remembered Thompson. Yohe placed the bottle upon the bar and poured Thompson a shot. Thompson downed the shot, and Yohe cleared the bar. Thompson then said to Yohe that he had heard that he could whip any man in Mt. Jewett. Yohe replied that he was not a fighter but would defend himself if he was run on. Thompson then asked Yohe how much he weighed, and Yohe said one hundred and fifty pounds. Thompson said he weighed one hundred and fifty-one pounds, and he would fight Yohe for $100 on Monday. Yohe said he was not a fighting man and asked Thompson to pay for his drink. Thompson paid the money and then said he was going to run the whole house. Yohe said he was there to run the bar and that Thompson had been troubling him enough and pointed towards the door. Two patrons then entered the bar and ordered bottles of beer. Yohe poured their beer into glasses, and in the act of setting the bottles back under the bar, he told Thompson to leave the bar once again. Thompson drew a revolver out of his vest, and point-black shot Yohe, who still had his hands behind the bar. Yohe staggered back into the hallway behind the bar and collapsed.

Thompson briskly walked out of the bar bypassing the daughter of the owner, Ms. Nellie Brewer, who stood in his path. He then brandished his pistol into the face of J. E. Conley, a young civil engineer who tried to stop him from leaving the bar. Thompson took off down Main Street while the news quickly spread that he had shot young Yohe. Yohe had been carried onto a bed in the hotel but died before a medical doctor arrived. Close to one hundred men soon gathered about the Brewer House, but all were reticent to confront Thompson, who was seen roaming in the distance with his pistol at his side. As Mt. Jewett did not have a police force, the men sent a notice to Smethport about the shooting and that the murderer was loose on the streets of Mt. Jewett and still armed. Thompson's employers in Mt. Jewett, Tennant & Johnson, were notified that their employee had committed a murder, and they sent Thompson's direct boss, Engineer White, to speak with the suspect. Thompson listened to the pleas of White to give himself up and finally allowed White to disarm him, and he agreed to head towards Smethport and the Sheriff's office. Thompson told White that he had thought Yohe had been reaching for a gun when he put the bottles behind the bar, as he did not leave the bar when asked. He said he shot first to not let Yohe get the drop on him and considered it in self-defense. Halfway to Smethport, the White group was intercepted by a posse led by Deputy Sheriff Clarke, and they took custody of Thompson and escorted him to the Smethport jail.

The coroner's inquest was held at the Brewer's House conducted by A. Y. Jones of Kane, who was standing in for Coroner Dempsey. They found that the bullet that struck Yohe had entered his left side and nipped his intestines and lungs. Yohe had died as a result of shock and blood loss. It was noted that Yohe had not received medical attention after the shooting and had expired forty-five minutes after being shot. Yohe had made no statements while he was dying. After hearing from a few witnesses, the jury rendered the verdict that the deceased came to his death from a pistol shot willfully administered by John E. Thompson. The remains and possessions of Yohe were then sent to his parent's farm in Reynoldsville. A mass was held at the Syphrit Church near there, and Yohe was buried in the church cemetery.

While Thompson sat in the Smethport prison, the men of Mt. Jewett swore vengeance. There was talk of breaking into the jail and lynching Thompson, but fairer heads prevailed, and the men decided to let justice prevail.

Thompson had come to Mt. Jewett from Lawrence County, where he had a wife and two children who lived in Wardensville. He had been the foreman of the P. & W. Railroad there but had been fired for drunkenness the previous winter. He was currently under bail from that county for slander. Thompson was a veteran of the civil war and had received a severe fracture of the skull from which he had never fully recovered. It was said that one drink of liquor always made him insane due to this injury. Thompson also reportedly said he had killed two men before and had been cleared of the charges later; whether this was true was not known. Thompson was middle-aged, well built, with a sandy complexion and a temper popularly coupled with red hair and a red mustache. He had been employed as the foreman by Tennant & Johnson that January to direct the completion of their new line being built between Mt. Jewett and Ormsby.

The seriousness and consequences of his actions caused Thompson to contemplate what really mattered in life. He wrote endless letters to his wife and children and attended religious services whenever they were offered in prison. His case was taken up in the December term of court in front of Judge Olmsted in the McKean County Courthouse. The only argument from the defense was for leniency and not to find their client guilty of first-degree murder. The case went to the jury, and for several hours, nine voted for second-degree murder while three held out for first-degree murder and the penalty of death. The majority finally convinced the three holdouts to spare the defendant's life, and they returned with a verdict of guilty in the second-degree. Judge Olmsted sentenced Thompson to a term of eleven years and six months in the Allegheny Penitentiary. This sentence was considered by many to have been too light of a sentence, with calls for the prisoner's execution growing. Word reached Sheriff Bannon that men in Mt. Jewett were preparing to hijack the train carrying Thompson when it passed through there and to perform some frontier justice with a good old hanging. Bannon decided to postpone the transfer of Thompson to Pittsburgh and instead sent word to Mt. Jewett that Thompson had been transferred to Pittsburgh the day after the trial and was now out of their grasps. The men in Mt. Jewett were incensed that Thompson had escaped their justice. Sheriff Bannon then waited until December 28th and assisted by Chief McCrea of Bradford and several deputies, put Thompson on a train and safely traveled through Mt. Jewett. When the train was over an hour past Mt. Jewett, Bannon sent word that Thompson was safely on his way to Pittsburgh. The Mt. Jewett gang was once again livid with the Sheriff and told reporters that had they known Thompson was on that train, he would never have passed through alive. Thompson reportedly was very nervous until they passed Mt. Jewett and then relaxed and slept the rest of the way to his new home for the next eleven plus years.

Feeble Minded

Little Ruby Gemmel was buried in the Degolia Cemetery.

Polk Center for the Feeble-Minded was where children and adults with mental retardation were sent to live for many years up to and including the middle of the last century. Horror stories could be written from the experiences of some of the residents who had been placed there against their will. Whether the center provided treatment or just confinement for these disabled individuals is a question that has never been fully answered. Today there are so many other treatments and living options for the mentally challenged, and centers like Polk are no longer considered humane, much less a viable treatment option.

In 1920, a West Bradford youth, Leo (*Gemmel*) Kelly, was adjudged to be feeble-minded and a juvenile delinquent and sent to the Polk Center in Venango County for treatment. Leo, who was sixteen, was the adopted son of James (*Jack*) Gemmel, who had married his mother. Leo was the child of Mrs. James Gemmel's previous marriage in Canada. This was Leo's second trip to the institution, and he fought the constables when they came to escort him to the center. Leo was a wayward youth who was easily influenced and had been caught committing petty crimes throughout the Bradford area. Older boys, knowing his intelligence was limited, would make criminal suggestions and Leo would obey. At sixteen years of age, Leo's thought process was one of a six-year-old who was in a teenage muscular body. Many who met Leo were fooled by their initial impression that he was just another teenager. Leo, however, had a problem with knowing the difference between right and wrong and was known to become extremely angry when he was corrected for even the slightest infraction. Leo looked for every opportunity to escape from Polk, and one sunny day in May of 1920, he found an opportunity when he was on a group walk through the fields. Leo slipped off unnoticed into the woods, and soon walked into the town of Franklin. In Franklin, he found a man traveling to Kane and who gave him a ride in an open carriage. In Kane, Leo had begged on the streets for money and a meal. Several generous people gave him a few dollars, which he used to purchase a train ticket to Bradford. Kelly reached Bradford by train and he walked the rest of the way to his parent's house, which was located near the Gilbert Reservoir on Willow Creek Road. He showed up at the house and noticed that his uncle Oliver's horse and buggy were in the barn. Leo decided to go for a ride instead of going into the house and momentarily was headed into town at the reigns of the buggy.

Oliver noticed his rig scurrying down the road and contacted the police in Bradford to report the theft of his carriage and horse. The next day, Thursday, May 6th, Oliver left the house in the morning in search of his property. While Oliver was out searching, Leo returned with the horse and carriage. His aunt Marjorie, who was also his sister, seeing that it was Leo who took the wagon, went in search of Oliver to tell him that the rig had been returned.

Living with the Gemmel's at this time was Oliver Gemmel, brother of James. Oliver had married the sister of Leo, Marjorie. As Leo was sitting on the front porch waiting for his uncle and sister to return, his stepfather James Gemmel came out of the house and proceeded to berate him. James called Leo a few choice words and also said Leo's mother was a fool to have kept such a child as him alive. Leo grew angry at the tongue lashing and ran into the house when James was done with his rant.

Leo was furious when he entered the house and quickly thought of how he could get even with his stepfather. Mr. and Mrs. Oliver Gemmel had been blessed with a beautiful baby girl nine months prior whom they named Ruby Adelia Gemmel. Leo had been living in the house when the baby was born and was jealous of the attention that the young baby had received from not only her parents but his parents as well As he was standing in the kitchen, he heard the baby Ruby crying from her crib upstairs, and then and there, he entered the realm of a truly criminal mind. Leo crept up the stairs and soon was looking down at the innocent face of the beautiful baby in her crib. Leo pulled a dull knife out of his pocket and began to saw slowly upon the neck of the infant. Due to the dullness of the blade, it took him several minutes to cut through the windpipe and jugular vein. The poor baby gasped for breath and was motionless in a few minutes. Leo then wiped off his knife and put it back into his pocket.

Kelly fled the home and had only made it down the road a short distance when he encountered Oliver and his sister, who were returning from their earlier search. Oliver halted the boy and made him return to the house, intent on questioning him about the theft of the horse and carriage. Oliver had no idea that Leo had just murdered his infant daughter. When they reached the house, they were met by a horrified James Gemmell, who told his brother what the young Leo had done.

Oliver Gemmell, full of grief and rage, showed great restraint in not taking Leo out and punishing him as most people would have. James held Leo while Oliver went to a neighbor's house, David McQuilkin, who had a phone. The Bradford police were notified, and soon one of the most horrible murders to ever have been committed in McKean County would be brought to the public's attention.

Police Chief Howe and Patrolman Foster could not believe what they were hearing on the phone. The police only had access to horses, and they wanted to get to the scene as quickly as possible. Knowing that the fastest way for them to reach the crime scene was by automobile, they went into the streets and commandeered the first auto they found. Howe and Foster were soon at the location where they found Leo being held in the custody of his stepfather.

The police put handcuffs on Leo and searched his body. They found the knife he had used to murder young Ruby in his pocket, along with chewing gum, cigarette papers, and odds and ends.

While on the way into the city, Leo asked Chief Howe:

"What will they do to me?"

"They ought to hang you!" the chief replied.

Kelly reportedly laughed and asked: "Do you think they will?"

When they arrived at the police station, Leo was taken into the interrogation room and was asked a further series of questions.

On a reason for the murder, Kelly offered no motive for his crime other than he was mad at Jack (James).

"Why did you kill the baby?" He was asked.

"Jack called me names. He called my mother names." Kelly muttered in reply. "I told him that I'd kill somebody if he didn't stop."

"But if you were angry at Jack, why didn't you kill him instead of the baby?"

"Jack is bigger than I am," the murderer replied.

"How long did it take you to kill the baby?" Chief Howe asked Kelly.

"Three minutes, maybe five minutes," Kelly answered without apparent emotion.

"Did she cry out?"

"No."

Kelly was then asked: "aren't you sorry you did it?"

The murderer hung his head for a moment.

"Yes," he said, almost inaudibly.

Kelly had shown little emotion during his examination by the police. But a few minutes after being taken back to his cell, he began to weep loudly. He called for Chief Howe and asked if he could see his mother and stepfather. The parents never showed up at police headquarters that night.

The tiny body of baby Ruby was taken to the Koch Undertaking Parlors for an autopsy and planned coroner's inquest. The victim was described as a beautiful, fair-haired child whose face showed no anguish despite the horrible trauma the baby went through. It was as if the child was simply asleep. The rest of her body, however, revealed the horrible truth. Upon the baby's throat was a terrible gash, one area wider than the other in the spot where the jugular vein was severed. On the left side of the breast was a deep wound where the defendant stabbed the infant, and beginning in the center of the abdomen and extending around the left side to the spine was a deeper gash, and it was believed that the knife had extended far into the body.

Coroner Heffner seated a jury which consisted of H. H. Adsit, Frank Zook, M. Roland, George Clough, E. W. Bisett, and M. L. Willis. The jury viewed the shattered body of Ruby then took their seats in the front of the room while the maniac who did this was brought into the parlors. The officers brought Leo into the room and told him to go right up to the coffin and look at what he had done. Leo gazed for a few minutes and put his hand up to his face and seemed to cry, but soon all traces of emotion left his face, and he stared blankly at the jury. The jury stared with horror at Leo, and it was easy to see that they would issue an order to have the prisoner arrested for the cold-blooded murder of this innocent, defenseless child. After a brief report of the cause of death of young Ruby by Coroner Heffner, and testimony by Chief Howe of the confession that Leo had given him, the jury pronounced that young baby Ruby Gemmell came to her death from knife wounds wielded by Leo (*Gemmel*) Kelly. Leo was taken back to Bradford and hastily transferred to the Smethport jail, facing a charge of first-degree murder. The day after the coroner's jury, services for the baby Ruby were held in Koch's Chapel, and she was buried in the Degolia Cemetery.

Leo's parents, meanwhile, were suffering from the most intense grief over what their son had done. While looking over the rig that Leo had taken that night, they noticed a bundle in the back which was wrapped in a blanket. Opening the bundle, they found many postcards, packages of gum, cigarette papers, and numerous other goods. The postcards were marked Degolia, and they remembered that there was a report of a burglary at the Degolia Post Office on the night that Leo stole the carriage. Leo was not only a murderer but a thief as well. They notified the police, who picked up the stolen goods and then turned them over to Mrs. Bishop, the postmistress of the Degolia Post Office.

Leo did not adapt well to the structured life at the county jail. He often ignored or refused commands and attempted to do as he liked. Prison officials also observed that Leo was not only of limited intelligence, but he was easily manipulated by fellow criminal elements who would dare him to do bizarre acts. He was observed to follow anybody's directions, no matter what the consequences. The prison warden contacted the district attorney and told him that they best get the prisoner examined by a mental health specialist as Leo did not act as though he was in charge of his own facilities'.

Dr. H. W. Mitchell, Superintendent of the Warren State Hospital for the insane, took the train to Bradford, where he was met by County Detective Allison. Mitchell traveled to Smethport in Allison's auto and promptly checked into the local hotel. Mitchell spent nearly a week in Smethport examining Leo as well as Harry Arnett, a youth charged with arson. Mitchell then prepared for the criminal trial of Leo, and his testimony as an alienist of note would be the most crucial evidence in determining whether Leo was put to death or whether he would be spared and sent to a state institution for life.

On June 7th, the case of the Commonwealth versus Leo Kelly was taken up in Smethport in front of Judge H. H. Heck. The jury trial was mostly limited to the testimony of Dr. H. W. Mitchell from the Warren State Hospital, who testified at length that Kelly was not only insane but a menace to society that should never walk the streets again. The jury, under instructions of Judge Heck, returned a verdict that Kelly was a lunatic and should be institutionalized. Judge Heck ordered Kelly's commitment to the State Hospital for the Insane at Fairview in Wayne County, never to be released into the public again. Kelly was taken back to his cell to await his transfer, but he was not going to go willingly.

On June 13th, while Kelly awaited transfer to Fairview, he attended church services with other inmates at the prison. At the service, several prisoners pointed to an open door at the side of the chapel and told Kelly to "beat it." Kelly took their advice and quickly ran from the prison and headed into town, where he hired a cab that took him to the railroad station. At the station, he bought a ticket to Bradford. He had received some money from his mother at a recent visit and had this money in his pockets when he had made his escape. Jail authorities quickly discovered Kelly had escaped, and bulletins were put out with his description. Law enforcement did not think Kelly had any money, so they headed towards Bradford on horseback hoping they would overtake him along the way. In Bradford, Luke Howe, son of the Chief of Police John Howe, happened to have been on a trolley when Kelly boarded. Howe had previously seen Kelly at the police headquarters after the murder and instantly recognized him. He kept an eye on Kelly until the car reached the corner of Main and High Street. Patrolman Fairbanks was on duty at that point, and young Howe called the officer who boarded the trolley and placed Kelly under arrest. Kelly was taken to the Bradford jail. Detective Allison arrived shortly, and Leo was soon back behind bars in Smethport, this time under a lockdown. On June 23rd, Kelly was finally taken by Sheriff Joseph Robinson to the Fairview Hospital for the Criminally Insane, where he ended his days. In my opinion, Kelly committed the most heinous murder in all of the four hundred plus cases I have researched.

Death at Kinzua

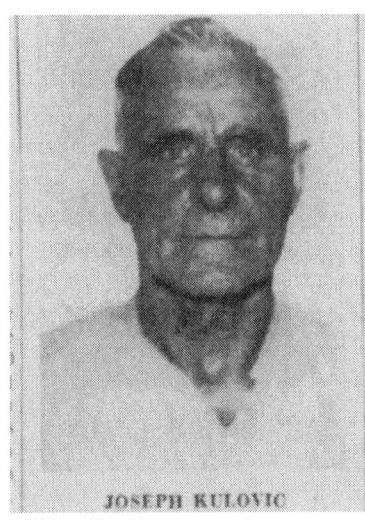
JOSEPH KULOVIC

The lives of lumbermen employed in back-breaking work often revolved around payday and the pursuit of alcohol when the workweek was over. Men employed in this profession worked long hours for low pay. Because of the remote location of their lumber camps, the only time they did come to town was to spend their money on alcohol and good times. Many of these lumbermen were also immigrants who spoke little English and were in this country without any nearby relatives. Their "family" was their fellow working men, and the camaraderie they shared sufficed for their need for familial relations.

Located about four miles from Kinzua, at Pigeon Run, Mike Eskra, a Kane area jobber, had a lumber camp deep in the woods. Eskra employed several woodcutters of Austrian heritage, and two of these men were Anthony Trenta and Joseph Kulovic. The camp consisted of small shacks in which two workers bunked in a double bed and spent their off times together. If a conflict arose between these bunkmates, Eskra would move them to another shack and he felt harmony amongst his workers was paramount to a successful lumber operation. Kulovic had been a long-term employee of Eskra, and when Eskra hired Trenta, he thought the logical bunkmate he should have would be Kulovic, as both of the men came from Austria. The arrangement seemed to progress harmoniously for the first two weeks. As was the custom in this lumber camp, payday meant the occupants that drank alcohol would go into either the towns of Warren, Bradford, or Kane to imbibe and celebrate the ending of their workweek. Payday on June 24th, 1955 was a well awaited and planned break from the lumber operation. Mr. Eskra offered a free ride to anyone who wanted to accompany him to Bradford. Kordish the camp truck driver also offered a seat in his truck and was traveling to the taverns of Kane. Kulovic went to Kane while Trenta traveled to Bradford with Eskra. Trenta had borrowed $20 from Kulovic as he had not cashed his paycheck yet and wanted to drink as soon as he got to Bradford. Trenta promised to pay Kulovic back once he returned from Bradford. Both of the men enjoyed their night out and returned to their shack at different times during the night. Mr. Kordish, the truck driver, arrived back with Kulovic, and they entered Kulovic's hut. Kordish saw Trenta hand Kulovic two $10 bills and then left the shack and headed back to his abode.

Trenta, who was intoxicated from his trip to town, walked away from Kulovic muttering to himself. He turned around with a knife in his hand and immediately went after Kulovic. Kulovic deflected the attack and was successful in securing the knife and used it to slash at the still attacking Trenta. Kulovic slashed Trenta several times in his chest, and Trenta then ran outside and grabbed an ax. The two were shouting at each other, and this drew the attention of Fred Yanish, the camp foreman, and Matt Kacele, a fellow woodcutter. They saw Trenta exit his shack and then grab an ax which he swung at the closely following Kulovic. The men grabbed the ax when Trenta started to swing again, and at that time, Kulovic slashed Trenta with the knife in his face with the blade penetrating along Trenta's nose. Trenta dropped the ax and ran around the shack with Kulovic in pursuit. Kulovic appeared again and went into his cabin, knife still in his hand and muttering to himself. The witnesses then went and looked for Trenta and found him bleeding to death behind the shack. The woodsmen notified the authorities that there had been a death at their lumber camp.

State Trooper William Wooditch of the Kane barracks arrived first to the lumber camp quickly followed by County Detective Gordon Foley and Assistant District Attorney Guy Mayo. Coroner Elmer Beatty had already arrived and pronounced Trenta deceased. Kulovic was taken into custody under suspicion of murder and transported to the county jail in Smethport, pending the results of the coroner's inquest. Coroner Beatty arranged for the removal of the body of Trenta to the Koch-Chatley Funeral Home, where an autopsy would be performed. Detective Foley remained on the scene and took witness statements. He gave these statements to Mayo to consider what, if any, charges would be placed against Kulovic.

Coroner Beatty held an inquest on Wednesday the 29th at the funeral home in Bradford. Dr. Leo Moss, the pathologist of Olean and Bradford hospitals, conducted the autopsy. Moss found that Trenta suffered knife wounds to his throat, deep wounds to his face, three cuts to the left arm, and a fatal knife thrust to the left side which broke a rib and penetrated the lung and heart. The heart wound had caused the death, having severed the aortic valve. Testimony was also received from Yanish and Kacele, who both witnessed part of the fight, but who did not see the actual stabbing which resulted in Trenta's death. Kulovic, in a short statement in broken English, claimed self-defense and said that Trenta became angry with him when he said he was going to move to another cabin. The inquest declared that Anthony Trenta came to his death at the hands of a knife wielded in the hands of one Joseph Kulovic. Kulovic was hastily arraigned before Justice of the

Peace Arnold Fields of Hazelhurst and returned to the county jail charged with first-degree murder in the death of Trenta.

The funeral service for Anthony Trenta was held at the Koch-Chatley Chapel in Bradford on July 1st. Trenta was born in Austria in 1897 and was fifty-eight years old when he died. He had been in the United States for many years and had worked in the lumber industry since coming to this country. Trenta was married; however, his wife was still in Austria, and a letter was sent to her from Coroner Beatty explaining the circumstances of his death. The only know relative of Trenta in the States was Tony Malecker of Cincinnati, Ohio. Trenta's remains were buried in St. Bernard's Cemetery in Bradford.

The trial of Joseph Kulovic for the murder of Anthony Trenta took place on October 6th, 1955, in the Smethport Courthouse. Assistant District Attorney Guy Mayo represented the Commonwealth while Attorney Glenn Mencer represented the defense. Judge Charles Hubbard presided.

The prosecution began their case by calling Dr. Leo Moss, the physician who performed the autopsy, as their first witness. Moss described the wounds inflicted upon the body of Trenta and explained that the knife wound that severed the aortic valve had caused Trenta to succumb to his death within several minutes due to loss of blood, which flowed into his body cavity.

Matt Kucele was then called. He said his shack was within twenty-five feet of the Kulovic shack and sounds of their argument had caused him to go outside to see what the arguing was about. Kucele said he witnessed Trenta grab an ax, and he and the foreman, Yanish, had grabbed the ax when Trenta made a second attempt to hit Kulovic. Kucele said that Kulovic then slashed at Trenta's face with his knife and that Trenta dropped the ax and ran behind the shack with Kulovic in hot pursuit with a knife in his hand. He did not witness the death of Trenta.

Miss Ruth Eskra, daughter of the owner of the lumber camp, then testified. She said she was driving back to camp and found the road at the camp blocked by a car near the Trenta-Kulovic shack. She said she looked toward the shack and saw Kulovic in the doorway with a knife in his hand. Mr. Yanish was on the porch, and Mr. Trenta was on the porch with an ax in his hand. She said the right side of Mr. Trenta's face was bleeding. Ms. Eskra said she jumped into Yanish's car and drove to the main camp to rouse her parents. Her father and mother returned to the shack and found that Mr. Trenta was no longer breathing. The prosecution then rested their case.

The defense then commenced and called Joseph Kulovic to the stand. Kulovic, through an interpreter, Mary Golemund of Lamont, in a calm manner, described his fight with Anthony Trenta. He said the fight broke out when he informed Trenta of plans to move out of the small shack they shared. He said Trenta, who was intoxicated, struck him with a hurled stone or piece of wood. Kulovic said he cut his bunkmate on the face with a butcher knife while trying to prevent him from reaching a go-devil, which is a chisel-like implement used for splitting wood. Kulovic asserted that he was too excited to remember all of the details of the battle, which ended in Trenta's death. Kulovic told the court that Trenta confronted him first with a knife, then with an ax. Defendant said the victim shared a double bed in the shanty for about two months before the fatal stabbing and that his actions on June 28th were in self-defense. Kulovic stated that he did not want to kill Tony because he had nothing against him. The defense then rested.

After the closing arguments of the prosecution and the defense, Judge Hubbard charged the jury with rendering a verdict. Hubbard pointed out specifically that Mayo had not asked for them to bring in a verdict of first-degree murder, which was the highest charge Kulovic faced. This was telling the Judge said, but it was their responsibility to return with either a verdict of guilty in the first degree, second degree, voluntary manslaughter, or acquittal. The jury then retired to discuss the case. The jury returned after six hours of deliberating and declared

Kulovic "not guilty" of murder. Kulovic was released from custody on a motion by Mayo and returned to his home in Kane for the first time since June.

Joseph Kulovic ended up retiring from the hard labor of woodcutting and lived out his life in Kane at his residence on Birch Street. He died there on Tuesday, May 12th, 1964, at age seventy-one. During his many years in the lumber industry, he had been employed as a woodcutter by Mrs. Rose Kocjancic, Michael Eskra, and Nick Novosel, Jr. He was a member of St. Callistus Catholic Church, where his funeral mass was celebrated by the Rev. Carl L. Lippert. Burial was in the St. Callistus Cemetery in Kane. He had no known survivors in this country.

Rubbed Out

The body of Mattafaro was dumped on the left side of the road near this sign to Lewis Run on Big Shanty Road.

During the prohibition years, Bradford was often called "Little Chicago" for very good reasons. Many men were gunned down and murdered over the precious liquid called alcohol. In a bitter war that took place in the 1920s between rival bootlegging gangs, as many as thirty men lost their lives in a triangle encompassing Olean, Bradford, Johnsonburg, and Warren. Most of these men did indeed die due to their involvement in this lucrative trade, but even ones who did not, such as Dominic Scopiletti of Johnsonburg (*Elk County Murders, Volume I*), ties to bootlegging were enough to include them as victims of the war. (*Scopiletti was cut up in 11 pieces, and this fact pretty much proved he was a victim of a crime of passion and not an actual underworld hit.*) The following is an account of just one individual who lost his life in this war, with many more accounts to follow in future books.

John (*Giovanni*) Mattafaro was a man on a mission. He was employed by Joe Barber as an enforcer, and according to reliable sources, Barber had been the bootlegging king who had ordered the deaths of over fifteen men in McKean and Cattaraugus Counties with ties to many more murders. Barber never actually killed anyone, he instead ordered the hits, and his enforcers unquestionably carried them out. It was reported to be just as dangerous to be his enemy as it was to have been his "friend." Whenever Barber barked a command, his soldiers listened and never came back without the deed being accomplished. Mattafaro had been called to the Barber residence on the night of January 7th, 1927, to complete one of these missions. Mattafaro, forty-two and a loyal soldier of Barber, had recently come under suspicion by Barber for alleged connections to another bootlegger, the infamous Patsy Mussolino, who had disappeared in 1925, never to be seen alive again. Even when a former rival was dead or missing, suspicion still followed their associates. Mattafaro had stopped to visit Mrs. Esther Mussolino with his new young wife, Camilla, and they stayed for several hours before Mattafaro told his wife he had to go get his car at Barber's house and go to work. Camilla was not sure what type of work her husband did, but she knew whatever it was, it paid the bills. She bid her beloved a good night and walked back to her residence, never realizing that this would be the last time she would see her husband alive.

Mattafaro went to the Barber residence and spent around an hour inside speaking with his boss, Mr. Joe Barber. Barber was given his orders for the mission and drove away from the residence as he did so many nights before with a duty to fulfill. A certain Della Pascarello saw Mattafaro near Kreinson's Store on Main Street in Bradford around 11 pm that night, but soon others would see Mattafaro, and they too would be on their own mission. Whether Mattafaro headed towards Olean, Salamanca, Lewis Run, or somewhere in between is a secret that was never discovered. Wherever his mission took him that night, he most certainly was entering a double-cross engineered by his boss Joe Barber. How he spent his final minutes can only be speculated on, but the resulting bullet wounds found in his head left no doubt that this was a sanctioned hit and one that was meant to silence Mattafaro forever.

On Friday, February 4th, 1927, Arthur Atkinson and Harry Foster spent that cold day pulling gas wells on Big Shanty Road outside of Lewis Run. Both men were employees of the W. C. Kennedy Oil Company and worked hard for their money. The month of January had dumped a large amount of snow in this area, but in the last few days, sunshine had started to melt some of the covering, while cold, stiff temperatures still prevailed. On their drive back to Lewis Run, the men stopped at a spring along the side of the road to get a drink of ice-cold water. As they quenched their thirsts and discussed the day, they both noticed an object which was about one hundred and fifty feet directly behind the spring. To the men, it appeared to be a bundle of clothes, but both knew it was something that did not belong in the woods. Walking up to the "bundle," the men were horrified when they saw it was not a pile of clothes but the body of a man, whose face was grotesquely disfigured. The body was fully dressed, and a fedora hat lay some four feet away from the body. The men saw old foot tracks in the snow around the body, along with numerous animal tracks. Both men hurried back to their truck to go and inform the authorities of their gruesome find. The men drove the mile to the Lewis Run gas station, where they phoned in their find to the Bradford Police. Soon the authorities were on the scene.

Bradford Police Detective Fairbanks took the call from Atkinson and briefly discussed the report with his department. The Bradford Police had a list of local missing persons which they kept hanging on the wall, and by the report that the body was frozen stiff but still whole, they at once suspected it could be John Mattafaro. Mattafaro had been reported missing in January by his new bride, and she had stopped into the station just the day before to inquire if they had any news on her husband. As Fairbanks and Patrolman Mike Ferko traveled to Lewis

Run, they also left word for McKean County Detective Jack Allison and County Coroner Heffner of the discovery.

Fairbanks and Ferko met Atkinson and Foster at the Lewis Run gas station, and the men led them to the body. Coroner Heffner arrived soon after. The body of the man lay partially frozen, and bullet wounds in the man's head were obvious. Parts of the man's face, including his nose and hands, were chewed on by what was suspected to have been rodents. They spotted what looked like footprints in the snow around the body, but they were older than Atkinson's and Fosters. There was no way of knowing how long ago they had been made, and no details could be ascertained from the tracks. They speculated that the body was carried to where it was found as there were no drag marks in the snow. The lack of blood around the wounds in the head pointed to the fact that the man was not killed where he was found. Papers on the body identified the dead man as one John Mattafaro, who lived at 125 Forman Street in Bradford. This was the man reported missing by his wife. Coroner Heffner ordered the body removed to Still's Funeral Home in Bradford, where an autopsy and coroner's inquest would be held. The police officers searched the area and were unable to find the weapon that killed the man. County Detective Allison and Bradford Police Chief Travis visited the scene later in the evening and using lights were also unable to find any additional evidence.

Detective Fairbanks called Mrs. Camilla Mattafaro into the Bradford station for questioning when they returned to their station. She was informed of the finding of her husband's body, and she wept uncontrollably for some time. She retold her story of having met Mattafaro around a year prior and said he had come from the Olean area and moved to Bradford within the past six months. Camilla, who was a mere seventeen years old, had married Mattafaro in Limestone, New York, only two weeks prior to his disappearance on January 7th. It was noted that Mattafaro was quite a bit older at forty-two years of age, and Camilla stated that she loved John, and that was all that mattered. Camilla also stated that Mattafaro had told her he had a wife and a twenty-year-old daughter in Italy. She said that she did not report her husband missing right away because she thought he might have simply deserted her. She recounted how she last saw her husband at Mussolino's that night, and he told her he was going to do work for Barber, and she never heard from him again. The detectives then began their investigation, but knowing the names of those involved, they did not have high hopes of solving this murder.

Coroner H. Clay Heffner called an inquest at the Still Funeral Home on Saturday morning, the day after the body was discovered. The body had been allowed to thaw in the funeral home on Friday night, and Dr. Joseph Kervin had performed the autopsy. Dr. Kervin found that there were four wounds to the head, all on the left side. One was about two inches in front of the ear, the bullet passing entirely through the head. Another was five inches above the left ear. This bullet was found in the base of the skull. The third was behind the ear; this bullet was found in front of the right ear. The fourth hole was in the neck, four inches below and behind the ear. The course of this bullet was traced and also was found behind the right ear.

Dr. Kervin said that any of these wounds would have caused almost instant death, and this ruled out any chance of suicide. Dr. Kervin also found a tattoo on the right forearm, which depicted a dagger and a serpent entwined upon the dagger. The words "Dolce Vendetta" in Italian were written below this tattoo. This phrase, translated into English, means "Sweet Revenge." The tip of the nose had been gnawed at by animals, and the right hand was disfigured by birds or squirrels which had been pecking and feeding on the exposed flesh. Kervin also said that there were powder burns around two of the holes, which indicated that the weapon was close to the head when the shots were fired. He found one hole in the man's hat and noted the other three were shot below the brim. Kervin speculated that the body had been dumped at the site where it was found soon after death due to the condition of the body, and he also speculated that it more than likely was the same night he had disappeared. After hearing the testimony of the men who had found the body and the authorities who had investigated the death, Heffner called upon the jury to make their decision. The jury returned the verdict that Giovanni (*John*) Mattafaro came to his death by shots fired by a .38 revolver by a person or persons unknown.

Detective Allison took over the investigation and contacted the Olean Police for their insight as Mattafaro and Barber had come from there. Olean offered the opinion that the death had no connection with a vendetta killing from the wife in Italy, and this motive was quickly dismissed. In interviews with Joe Barber, they met a stone wall, and Barber said they only knew each other in passing, and he would answer no other questions and lawyered up. Mrs. Mussolino said that Mattafaro was a dear friend and had only been at her house to introduce his new wife, and there was nothing that she could add to his murder. The mysterious Della Pascarello, who said they saw Mattafaro that fateful evening was never available for an interview and later denied telling young Mrs. Mattafaro that they had told her this information. The investigation into the death of Mattafaro encountered a wall of silence. This silence was something law enforcement anticipated whenever a figure connected to the bootlegging trade was murdered. The murder of Mattafaro was never solved.

The funeral services for Mattafaro were held at the Still Funeral Home chapel on February 9th, and he was buried in St. Bernard's Cemetery. Joe Barber reportedly sent flowers but did not attend. Ironically his teenage widow remarried two months later. I wonder if she had something to do with the murder. I also wonder if his car was ever found. It does not appear the auto was ever recovered and probably found a new home with a more favored member of the Barber syndicate. Ironically, Joe Barber also met his maker in 1931 and took all of his secrets with him to his grave after he too was "rubbed out."

Major Ashton

A picture of a wagon similar to Major Ashton's in old time Bradford.

In the Bradford of the early 1880s lived an African American man affectionately known as Major Ashton. Ashton had spent many years in Bradford gathering garbage from many of the local establishments, and this is how he made his living. News reports of the day described Ashton driving a dilapidated wagon throughout the streets, and he was followed by his tame black bear, who faithfully followed Ashton from business to business. Locals often stopped to pet this bear, and Ashton was proud of his bear and the attention he received whenever he appeared within the city limits. Bradford, which was only incorporated into a city in 1879, was already developing into a major oil-producing area by 1883. Murder and other serious crimes were practically unknown at this time, but as always, things were about to change as the recently discovered oil also brought many more people into the previously sleepy city. On an August day in 1883, Major Ashton, a local fixture, was about to become the first victim of homicide in the new city.

On Thursday, August 23rd, 1883, Major Ashton, followed by his faithful bear, was making his rounds in Bradford, picking up the garbage at his usual stops. Aston stopped at the Shadyside Saloon, located on Globe Street, for his regular pickup. Lounging in front of the Saloon were a bunch of men, including George Gordon, a man who had only recently moved to Bradford from Ridgway and who was not familiar with Ashton and his bear. Gordon had a pet hound with him, and seeing the bear, he set his dog upon the bear as a form of amusement. Aston, hearing the ruckus behind his wagon and seeing the fight between the dog and his beloved bear, attempted to separate the two animals. Aston became quite angry and yelled at Gordon to call his dog off. Gordon laughed and said he would not. Ashton then threatened Gordon and rushing in front of Gordon; he proceeded to slap Gordon in his face. The much smaller Gordon then began to run down an alley. Ashton picked up a rock and hurled it towards Gordon. Gordon drew a Smith & Wesson revolver he had secreted in his shirt and fired at Ashton. The first shot missed, and Gordon continued to retreat. Ashton picked up another rock, and Gordon fired a second-round that struck Ashton in the mouth. Gordon, although dazed, picked up another rock, and Gordon fired a third-round that went through Ashton's heart. The murderer ran and was eventually detained by the fire police who were in front of their station, preparing for their annual parade at the time of the shooting. The police were summoned and Gordon was transported to the city jail to await charges. A crowd of African Americans had already gathered, demanding that Gordon be lynched. Ashton had died almost immediately from the shot to his heart, and his body was taken to the Webster Undertaking Parlor to await a coroner's inquest. Ashton's bear was collected by the police, and a local farmer was found to care for the animal.

While Gordon remained in jail, a coroner's inquest was organized at the funeral home over the remains of Major Ashton. The jury chosen included G. B. McCalmont, foreman, Edward Sutherland, James A. Sutherland, James A. Lindsley, Joseph Bensinger, William B. Clark, and R. F. Woodard. The "herculean" figure of Ashton laid on a wooden board in front of the jury. Ashton appeared to have been asleep, with the only sign of outward violence was a small hole near the left nipple. Doctors A. M. Williams and W. I. Craig conducted the autopsy. They found that the shot to the mouth was superficial and caused no damage except for minor discoloration. The bullet hole in the left breast, however, passed through the heart, and death would have been within seconds. The witnesses to the altercation and shooting were then called.

Frank Wentworth was the first witness called. Wentworth said he observed Major Ashton drive along Globe Street with his bear tied to his wagon. He watched Ashton drive into the creek and dispose of garbage and then observed his wagon to stop in front of the Shadyside Saloon on Globe Street. Wentworth noticed several dogs barking at the bear and saw the confrontation between Ashton and Gordon, with Ashton striking Gordon upon the side of the head. He heard Gordon say, "I did not mean anything," and saw Gordon pull a revolver from his pocket. Ashton stooped down to pick up a stone. Just as Ashton raised the stone, Gordon shot him and ran. Ashton followed and threw a stone. Gordon dodged the stone and turned and fired once again at Ashton. Ashton then fell upon his stomach. Wentworth ran to his nearby home for cold water and upon returning, found that Ashton was beyond assistance. He watched Gordon run down Globe Street and then down Pine Street. He said the pair were about ten feet apart when the shots were fired, and that Ashton did not say anything after being shot. He did say that he heard Ashton say to Gordon twice, "Mister, don't be too fresh." Wentworth had never seen the shooter before this day.

Frankie Meadows, the proprietress of a local saloon, was called next to testify. Meadows said she heard loud talking that morning and saw Ashton and a strange man of color in a controversy. Ashton said, "you had better not kick him again!" meaning his bear. Gordon replied: "I will kick him and you too," and they had further words. At that time, Ashton jumped off the wagon and said, "I mean you, Mister.!" Gordon replied, "I meant no harm," and repeated it two or three times. Ashton slapped him in the face. Ashton advanced towards Gordon while Gordon stepped back. Gordon produced a revolver, fired quickly, and ran while Ashton picked up a stone and chased after him. Gordon turned his head over his shoulder and fired at Ashton, the latter at the same time throwing a stone. Ashton turned around, took two steps, and fell. Meadows did not see Gordon teasing the bear but did recognize Gordon. Gordon had been drinking the night before at her establishment and he had been called a cowboy by her bar patrons.

W. Coburn next testified that he was walking down Pine Street at about 10 am on that Thursday when he heard the cry of "police" and thought of "murder on Globe Street." He said he heard the cry for police several times and asked two fire policemen present to assist him. Someone said to him that the suspect was under the sidewalk. Coburn looked under the sidewalk planks and saw a foot and a leg. A. H. Weaver, one of the fire policemen, pulled Gordon out, and Gordon began to explain what had happened. Coburn and Weaver escorted Gordon to the city lockup. At the lockup, Gordon gave his revolver to Coburn. Coburn said the pistol had three balls in it, and two chambers were empty. The revolver was presented as evidence. Coburn said that Gordon refused to give his name.

After several more individuals testified to roughly the same story, the jury retired to render their decision. The coroner's jury returned in short order and pronounced that Major Ashton had come to his death by a revolver in the hand of one George Gordon. Gordon was ordered to be held pending formal charges to be filed by the district attorney. Gordon was then placed upon a train to be taken to the county jail in Smethport to await further action.

Major Ashton had come to Bradford from Owego, New York some years previously, and proceeded to establish his junk hauling business as well as a soap-making venture. He was said to have been forty-three years old in 1883 and a large, strong man, towering over six feet. Ashton reportedly lived with a white woman, some two miles from the city limits in a secluded area. Rumors were that he had a substantial fortune. The rather large group of people of color and indeed the white population considered Ashton a local icon, and his death was mourned by all the people of Bradford. His closest friends descended upon the undertaking parlor and told the proprietor that Ashton had a small fortune and should be buried in the best coffin available. Ashton's remains were placed in a $250 coffin *($6,500 in today's money)*, and the Webster rooms were full of mourners and curiosity seekers for an entire day. Investigations the next day found that Ashton was penniless, and there would be no one able to pay for this expensive casket. Webster transferred the remains into a plain pine box. The funeral procession proceeded to the African M. E. Church (*Copeland Chapel*), and the Reverend R. H. Jackson provided the eulogy. Burial took place in the Oak Hill Cemetery on Saturday, August 25th, 1883.

George Gordon continued to languish in the McKean County jail, and sentiment in the Bradford community tended towards breaking into the jail and delivering street justice via a hanging. Gordon was described as being thirty-two years old with multiple physical and mental deformities. Gordon had a humpback, and his intellect was more in tune with that of a child than an adult. On the Saturday that Major Ashton was murdered, he had been in Bradford for only one day, having arrived in Bradford from Ridgway the prior evening. Gordon was brought to Bradford from the McKean County jail following the coroner's inquest for a hearing in front of Alderman McClure. His attorneys waived the reading of the evidence collected at the coroner's jury and introduced a plea of "not guilty" for their client. Gordon answered several questions posed to him in a dazed and confused manner. A large contingent of the colored population of Bradford had gathered both inside and outside of the courtrooms and was heard demanding justice for Ashton. Gordon was ordered held on the charge of murder and squirreled out of the rear entrance to the courthouse and back to the Smethport jail.

The trial of George Gordon for the murder of Major Ashton commenced at the Smethport Courthouse on Tuesday, February 26th, 1884. District Attorney McSweeney represented the Commonwealth while Attorneys W. W. Mason and Eugene Mullin represented the defense. The jury chosen included C. C. Cooper, Sylvester Breckenridge, Christian Herzog, J. S. Hodges, C. H. Callenbecker, William Titus, John McCleary, Wm. Windsor, J. C. Gabbarro, Thomas Braddock, and Miles Crossmire.

The prosecution began by informing the jury that George Gordon did indeed shoot and kill Major Ashton on Thursday, August 23rd, 1883, in the city of Bradford. The prosecution acknowledged that the much larger Ashton had accosted the smaller and disfigured Gordon due to the latter picking on his bear. The question for the jury was whether the killing of Ashton by Gordon was justified in self-defense or an extreme overreaction and, therefore, a criminal act. The defense argued that the shooting of Ashton was an act of self-defense, and Gordon did not deserve any sentence as Ashton was the aggressor and struck the first blow.

McSweeney presented the same witnesses that testified at the coroner's jury. Upon cross-examination, the prosecution witnesses admitted that Ashton did strike Gordon first. Even after Gordon fired a wild shot that missed Ashton, Ashton continued to hurl a rock at Gordon. The premise of self-defense was thoroughly pressed as Mullin described the immense figure of Ashton, who accosted the pathetic figure of Gordon who had a humpback and was barely five feet in height.

The jury, after listening to the final arguments of both sides, retired at 10:10 in the morning and returned from the anteroom in an hour. The verdict was handed to the prothonotary who read the verdict. The jury found Gordon not guilty of the murder of Ashton, and he was ordered released from the confines of the jail where he had been incarcerated since August of the previous year. Gordon left the courthouse a free man and departed for parts unknown after thanking his attorneys and the jury.

Was justice served in this case? Public sentiment immediately after the shooting was totally against Gordon, and he certainly would have been lynched had he not been placed behind bars. As the months progressed before the trial, Gordon became an object of pity due to his deformities and the fact that his intellect was limited. Most citizens did not believe he would be sentenced to death for the shooting; however, most also wanted to see him serve some prison time for killing a much-loved fixture of Bradford's culture. Gordon disappeared from the area after the trial, and his eventual whereabouts were never reported. Ashton, however, appears to have continued to visit Bradford as a spirit. Wild accounts persisted in Bradford in the months following his murder in which he was seen to still ride his now ghostly wagon through "Pig Island" in the evening hours looking for trash to pick up and followed by his faithful bear. The woman whom Ashton lived with also reported that the spirit of Ashton had visited her one night and calmed a crying baby she could not comfort. Many who had known Ashton said he had a peculiar whistle whenever he came around to pick up the trash. This whistle was reported to have been heard for years after the slaying, always within the confines of Pig Island.

Dementia

The tombstone of Merle and Rena Backus in the Rose Hill Cemetery. The spelling of "Murl" was never used in any of his papers and it is wondered if perhaps it was a mistake.

Many people have dealt with aging parents and the struggle to keep them safe and in their own homes instead of the dreaded nursing home. Back in the 1920s, nursing homes did not exist, and instead, the poor folk's farm or a state institution for mental health were the only options for an aged parent exhibiting signs of dementia. Then as now, children would move into the elderly parent's residence to assist and care for the parents who had taken care of them when they were younger. From my experience, dealing with an elderly parent requires patience and nurturing. Some of the actions that a parent with dementia exhibits could at best be described as bizarre but totally to be expected.

Mrs. Mary Backus of Smethport was struggling to live alone at the age of eighty-three. Having been a widow for some time, she had recently been more forgetful than usual, and neighbors and friends noticed the marked confusion she was exhibiting and had informed her son, Merle, who was living in Bradford with his wife. Mrs. Backus was a member of one of the oldest and most prominent families of the Smethport area. Merle and his wife Rena soon moved into the mansion to look after Mary and to help her with the upkeep of the large residence. *(The Backus mansion where Mary lived was eventually torn down, and the "Hub" now occupies the lot directly across from the courthouse.)*

With the addition of her son and her daughter-in-law, Mary was able to continue living in her house, and although there were struggles, Merle knew he had done the right thing by moving back to his childhood home. Mary was declining every day and often accused her son and especially his wife of hiding and stealing the most irrelevant objects such as combs and toothbrushes. Patience was at a premium when situations like these arose.

On November 7th, 1924, Rena Backus was cleaning an upstairs bathroom and had removed a soiled piece of oilcloth from the room and intended to throw it away. Mrs. Backus was observing everything that Rena was doing and at once objected to her intent on throwing away the soiled oilcloth. Rena tried to explain to her elderly mother-in-law that the cloth was worthless and needed to go into the garbage, but Mary insisted that it should stay put. The two argued, and eventually, Rena stuffed the cloth into a garbage bag while Mary retired to her room. Mary went into a bureau where she kept a pistol and returned to the bathroom, where she pointed the loaded gun at Rena. Rena, seeing the pistol in Mrs. Backus's hands, attempted to wrestle the gun from her grasp, and the gun went off with the bullet striking Rena in the heart. Rena screamed and ran down the stairs and out onto the front porch, where she collapsed. The gunshot was heard by passerby, who hurried towards the residence just in time to see Rena exit the front door and collapse on her front porch. They attempted to talk with her, but her voice was incoherent before she succumbed to the loss of blood. Merle was just pulling a truck into the garage when he heard the shot, and he too ran to the front porch, but his wife had expired before he had a chance to speak with her. Rena's dress was smoking where the bullet entered, showing it had been fired at close range.

The authorities soon arrived, and Rena Backus was declared deceased. County Detective J. J. Allison took over the investigation, and County Coroner H. Clay Heffner removed the body of Rena to the H. H. Sasse Funeral Home in Smethport. An autopsy discovered that the bullet had entered the left chest near the heart and had severed several major veins causing Rena to bleed to death. Death was within one to two minutes after the shot was fired. Heffner formed an inquest and went to the Backus residence with Allison to interview Mrs. Backus. Mrs. Mary Backus, who was hard of hearing and used a horn to assist her, told the officials that she and her daughter in law had quarreled over an oilcloth and that she had only retrieved the pistol to scare Rena into leaving the oilcloth where it originally was. She said when she pointed the pistol at Rena, Rena had grabbed her hand, which held the pistol, and it had fired by accident. Due to her advanced age and condition, Allison decided against jailing the woman and instead had two state policemen guard her in her residence to make sure she did not leave. The house was searched beforehand, and all weapons were removed from the residence.

Mrs. Rena Ostrander Backus was born in Oneonta, New York, to John and Addie Ostrander in 1889. She had met Merle Backus when he was stationed there as an agent for the Atlantic Refining Company. Funeral services were held at both the Backus mansion and St. Luke's Episcopal Church in Smethport. She was buried in the Rose Hill Cemetery.

The coroner's jury met Saturday night, and after reviewing the autopsy report and the statement of Mrs. Backus and several bystanders who witnessed Rena's death, they ruled that Mrs. Merle Backus was killed during an alleged scuffle with Mrs. Mary Backus, the result of a disagreement over a piece of oilcloth. District Attorney E. G. Potter then had Justice of the Peace Gleason hold a brief hearing with Mrs. Mary Backus, where she was formally charged with the murder of her daughter-in-law, and afterward, Mary was returned to her residence.

On December 8th, 1924, the grand jury met in Smethport and found a true bill against Mrs. Mary Backus in the murder of her daughter-in-law, Mrs. Rena Backus. Mrs. Backus had already been pronounced unsound mentally, and it was expected that the court would instruct the jury, after hearing the evidence as to her mental state, to find her insane.

District Attorney Potter presented the case for the Commonwealth and laid out the details of the shooting and the evidence that the state had found regarding the defendant's mental state. He then turned the case over to the defense, who called Dr. W. A. Ostrander, Dr. Robert Hamilton, Dr. Burg Chadwick, Hon. J. W. Bouton, Rev. W. E. Van Dyke all of Smethport, and the main witness, Dr. H. W. Mitchell of the Warren State Hospital for the Mentally Insane. All of the witnesses testified to the peculiarities shown by Mrs. Backus, and Dr. Mitchell testified that Mrs. Mary Backus was, in his opinion, a dangerous character and not fit to be allowed at large. The jury was then charged by Judge Heck to return a not guilty verdict by insanity, which they duly agreed to. Judge Heck then committed Mrs. Mary Backus to incarceration in the North Warren State Hospital for the Insane for treatment. If and when she was declared sane, she would be returned to the court to face the first-degree murder charges, which were put on hold during her incarceration.

Mrs. Mary Backus was transported to the hospital by her son J. C. Backus, a famous local inventor and manufacturer, who owned the Smethport Novelty Company. Mr. Backus said his mother, who was so prominent in the Smethport community, retained her composure when she was admitted to the asylum, never to regain her freedom. The Backus family defrayed the expense of her care while she was in Warren.

The Backus family was one of the most prominent in the Smethport part of the state. The late husband of Mrs. Backus, Major John C. Baucus, fought in the civil war and was one of the best-known attorneys in that section. Her son, J. Clayton Backus, was the inventor of pin setting machines used in bowling alleys throughout the country. A daughter, Mrs. Lucy Seger, was a famous movie actress in New York City, who went under the stage name of Lucia Backus Seger. Mrs. Backus also had a son Fred W. Backus who was a lawyer in Olean, a son Merle at home, and a daughter Mrs. Nellie Cutler of Oneonta, New York.

The venerable lady, Mrs. Mary Windsor Backus, passed away at North Warren State Hospital on April 3rd, 1930. Her body was returned to Smethport and buried in the family plot at the Rose Hill Cemetery. This, however, was not the last tragedy to be inflicted upon this once great family. Tragedy seemed to follow the Backus family. Mary Backus had a son, Harold, who was killed in 1913 in the first fatal car accident in Smethport, when he hit a pole on Main Street. Her son Frank had died suddenly of a heart attack in 1919, and another son, Fred, had committed suicide in 1925, after being diagnosed with terminal cancer of the mouth. Another son George had died young, which left only J. Clayton, Merle and two daughters surviving. J. Clayton Backus succumbed to pneumonia in 1931, leaving only the widowed Merle as the surviving child in Smethport.

On November 7th, 1932, the eighth anniversary of his wife's death, Merle (Murl) Backus, forty-nine, placed a pistol to his right temple and pulled the trigger. Merle had been suffering from depression ever since his wife's death and could no longer face this world. He was buried alongside his beloved wife in the Rose Hill Cemetery.

Madness

Rosa's grave in St. Gabriel's Cemetery in Port Allegany.

Domestic violence is and has been a scourge throughout the world. Law enforcement is often unable to intervene in these types of situations, and if you ask any police officer, these are some of the most dangerous incidents that they have to respond to. Great strides in the protection of women and men suffering from domestic violence have taken place since the 1920s, when this incident took place, and mental health treatment has also greatly expanded.

On Sunday morning, March 25th, 1928, two daughters of Salvatore and Rosa Caputo of Port Allegany *(who went by the names of Mike and Rose Ross)* returned to their home after church services. The girls entered their house and were greeted by a suspicious silence. The girls were expecting activity in their house, especially from their mother, who usually cooked a large Sunday dinner. The girls yelled out for their mother and father. They entered the kitchen and were horrified to find the body of their mother lying in a pool of blood on the floor. They attempted to rouse their mother and quickly noticed she was deceased. The girls called for their father and when they did not get a reply, they ran outside and to a neighbor's house for help.

County Detective Jack Allison of Smethport was notified of the shooting at around noon on Sunday and immediately headed towards Port Allegany. After talking with the authorities at the crime scene, he took the description of the suspect and began canvassing the area. At a local gas station, he found a witness who identified Mike Ross as a man who had come to the station earlier and had hitched a ride in a car traveling towards Olean.

Allison called the Olean and Bradford police stations and notified the officers to be on the lookout for Salvatore Caputo alias Mike Ross who was wanted on the suspicion of first-degree murder of his wife.

The Olean police began to scour the streets of Olean and divided up into two search parties. Police visited the residence of Mrs. Angelo Sanzo, who was a sister of Ross, and learned that Ross was there but had left thirty minutes before they arrived. Mrs. Sanzo did not know that Ross was suspected of killing his wife. Police then traced Ross to Mansueto Cappelletti's residence on Coleman Street, where they were informed, he had left fifteen minutes earlier. On North Union Street, a man who knew Ross stated that he had passed Ross going toward North Olean about ten minutes before. Officer Blakeslee took this tip and called for backup. Officer Randall started down First Street while Blakeslee went towards the intersection of First and North Union Street to head off the man that he suspected of being Ross. Ross was captured near St. John's Roman Catholic Church on North Union Street by Officer Randall. In his pockets, police found two .32 caliber revolvers and several loose cartridges. Ross readily identified himself as the suspect and admitted he had killed his wife. Ross also made the statement that he was "Glad he did it!" Ross was taken to the Olean police station, and Detective Allison was notified of the arrest of the suspect. Ross was also noted to be visually intoxicated and appeared to be in some type of demented state. The officers noted that Ross had exhibited some quite "queer" actions when arrested, which they did not clarify.

Detective Allison was soon in Olean and interviewing Salvatore Caputo alias Mike Ross. Ross said that he was seated in the kitchen of his home and was arguing with his wife about her relations with other men. Ross said that he knew his wife was with a certain male that past Thursday and had spent the day with him. Mrs. Ross denied everything and told her husband he was crazy. Ross claimed that his wife threatened to have him arrested. Ross said he then took his wife by the shoulder and asked her, "Rosa, would you have me arrested?" Rosa answered, "You're right, I would!" Ross said that he then drew his revolver out of his pocket and shot once at her. Rosa did not fall and yelled, "Don't you kill me, Mike!" Ross said he shot her again, and she fell. He said he then went out the door and bummed a ride to Olean. Ross was once again quoted as saying, "I'm glad I did it!" Allison then took Ross back to Smethport and lodged him in the county jail pending formal charges being filed.

The body of Rosa Caputo (*Rose Ross*) was transferred to the Gallup Funeral Home in Port Allegany, where Acting Coroner Dr. S. A. McCutcheon held an inquest over the body on Monday evening. The inquest found that Rosa had been struck by a .32 bullet in the left lung, which had caused great damage to the blood vessels, and death had been within minutes while she had bled out. The findings of the inquest were that Rosa Caputo had come to her death by a gunshot wound fired by Salvatore Caputo (*alias Mike Ross*) on Sunday, March 25th, in Liberty Township near Port Allegany. District Attorney Charles Hubbard filed first-degree murder charges against Salvatore Caputo. He was arraigned in front of Justice of the Peace R. C. Gleason on Monday evening in Port Allegany, where he pled guilty to the charge. He was returned to the county jail until a grand jury was convened in June.

Rosa Caputo (*Rose Ross*) was born in Italy in 1885 and was forty-three years old when she was murdered. She was the second wife of

Caputo and had been married to him for twenty-three years. They were the parents of six children, three of whom were deceased. A funeral mass was held for Rosa at the St. Gabriel's Roman Catholic Church in Port Allegany, and her remains were buried in the St. Gabriel Catholic Cemetery outside of the town.

Detective Allison continued his investigation into the murder. He spoke with the neighbors and the employer of Ross. All of the neighbors stated Mrs. Caputo had an impeccable reputation, and none believed she could ever have been having an affair with any man. The neighbors did, however, say they had noticed Mr. Caputo acting very strangely as of late and questioned his sanity. He had been observed outside of his house without clothes on and had been talking to himself. His former employer, the Shawmut Railroad, had relieved him of his longtime position a month before the murder on account of his acting strangely at work. Allison took this information to the district attorney, who informed the jail to observe Ross's actions in the county lockup for strange and bizarre behavior.

The grand jury met in June of 1928 and found a true bill against Salvatore Caputo (*Mike Ross*) in the murder of his wife. Reports of the insanity of Ross had been supplemented in the materials that the grand jury reviewed, and any formal hearing was delayed until experts examined Ross in the jail and provided their report to the court.

Dr. Mitchell, noted alienist from North Warren State Hospital, examined Ross in the Smethport jail and provided a report and testimony to the court in December in front of Judge Bouton. Dr. Mitchell relayed that he believed Ross was suffering from alcoholic psychosis, chronic paranoid type, and was hopelessly insane and not in charge of his facilities and would not have been at the time of the murder. The court and jury agreed that Ross was insane, and he was committed to treatment in the North Warren State Hospital until and if he was deemed sane, at which time he would be brought back to McKean County to face the murder charges he had pled guilty to.

Salvatore Caputo was transferred to Warren State hospital and only left that institution in a simple pine box when he died on January 15th, 1938, of chronic myocarditis. He was seventy-two years old. Caputo's body was taken to Butler, Pennsylvania, where he was buried, far away from the remains of his unfortunate wife.

Missing in Ludlow

Windfall Run in Ludlow.

To lose a child to illness or an accident is something a parent never gets over. The loss follows them every moment of every day. Children are not supposed to die before their parents, and every time I see this happen, my heart melts for the parents left behind. The worst scenario would be losing a child to abduction. Never knowing what happened to that child or whether they were dead or alive would be a nightmare come true. The case of Marjorie West is well known in the McKean County area, but she was not the only child to have gone missing. Little Michael Steffan, who was just seven years old, was presumed abducted from Ludlow back in 1910. The story of his disappearance is still haunting to this day, coupled with the fact that another young lad disappeared on the same day, thirteen miles away in Lamont. (*Elk County Murders Volume II, Missing in Highland*). In my continuing research, I have found similar disappearances in Ridgway and in Potter County during this time period. It leads me to assume a white slavery group may have been operating in this area at that time. Too many coincidences make these disappearances appear to have been connected.

On Saturday morning, April 14th, 1910, seven-year-old Michael Steffan planned to go fishing in a small native trout stream near his family's farm in Ludlow. Michaels friend, George Ankovitch, was going to join him, and they planned to fish all day. On this Saturday, the weather was quite sunny and warm, which was a welcome relief from the winter weather that had kept the area blanketed in snow since November. The stream the boys were fishing was called Windfall Run, a small stream that had holes barely deep enough to go for a swim but deep enough to hold some nice trout. The boys fished until about noon. Ankovitch, who was older than Steffan, went ahead of the lad to sneak up on a big hole. He was only separated from Steffan for a short period when he went back to find his playmate. He was surprised to find no trace of the boy and no sign that he was anywhere on the stream. Ankovitch spent time walking back up the stream to where the boys had started fishing but still could not find Steffan. Ankovitch figured his buddy must have gone home, and he also decided to end the day and went to his house. He later went to the Steffan farm to find his friend to play, and that is when he found out that young Michael had never returned home.

Thirteen miles away in Lamont, Elk County, four boys were also fishing on this sunny day. Edwin Adams, nine years old, had accompanied three other older boys from his small village, and they fished a native trout stream leading from Lamont. In the afternoon, they had encountered a "wild man" who appeared in the bushes and who began to yell and chase the lads. The boys all ran towards Lamont; however, Edwin was unable to keep up, and the last the boys saw of him, he was losing ground to the stranger. The boys quickly reported the incident to Edwin's father, who was the foreman of the United Natural Gas Company in Lamont. Mr. Adams roused all of his employees, and a search began at once for the boy.

In Ludlow, Mr. Steffan, who was employed at the Curtis Leather Company at that place, notified his employer that his son was missing while fishing, and the employer released one hundred men from the plant to search the stream for the boy. The group inspected every inch of tiny Windfall Run but failed to find any trace of the lad. The next day, the leather company ordered all four hundred employees of their operations to search for the boy, and they were joined by every able-bodied man in Ludlow. Once again, these searches proved fruitless. As the weather had taken a sharp turn on Saturday night with freezing rain and snow, the searchers realized that a small boy with only light clothing covering him would not be able to survive long in this inclement weather.

Meanwhile, in Lamont, the search was joined by three hundred prison inmates from New York who had volunteered to search for young Edwin. Mounted State Police troopers also came, and the search party numbered well over one thousand men. Bloodhounds were also brought in but were unsuccessful in finding any scent of the boy beyond where his companions had last seen him. It was surmised that this most definitely was a kidnapping, and as Mr. Adams was a man of means, speculation was that he would soon receive a ransom note. One such note was indeed found pinned to a tree along the very stream that Edwin had disappeared from; however, this was later ruled a hoax. Searchers continued their task for several weeks after Edwin's disappearance, but no trace of him was ever found.

The searchers in Lamont switched their time between there and Ludlow. Windfall Run was dammed up at the headwaters to effectively drain the stream, but no trace of Michael was found. The searchers also dragged the holes of the larger Two Mile Run into which Windfall Run emptied with no success. It was said that every cave and crevice for miles was also searched in the hopes that the young Michael had wandered into the woods and later sought shelter in a cave from the inclement weather.

The Elk County Commissioners soon offered a $500 reward for the successful locating of the Adams boy; however, the McKean County Commissioners did not follow suit. The McKean Commissioners felt that it would be against the law for them to use county funds for such a reward and were harshly criticized for their inaction. Professor Burdett Bayle, Superintendent of the McKean County Schools, decided to step in. He organized a drive to raise a $1,000 ransom for the recovery of the body of young Michael Steffan at the end of May 1910. Professor Bayle had watched the case with interest from the start and scolded the commissioners for their inaction. Superintendent Bayle was unsuccessful in his venture, raising only $225 towards the goal, and he abandoned it. The McKean County Commissioners finally stepped forward in June and did offer the $500 reward, matching the Elk County Commissioners, perhaps after much pressure from the public and the newspapers.

While the search for the Adams boy continued for several months and hope remained that he would be found alive, the consensus in Ludlow and McKean County was that the Steffan boy was deceased. This discrepancy was pretty much explained by the lack of funds of the Steffan family versus the relatively means of the Adams family. Mr. Adams was able to use his considerable wealth to investigate every avenue to find his child, while the poor Steffan family had very little cash at their disposal. Mr. Adams hired a clairvoyant to assist, and she told him that the boy was taken by a foreigner who spoke little English. This resulted in many searches of foreigner's residences in Elk County for signs of the boy. Whenever a report came from afar of a young boy matching Edwin's description, Mr. Adams traveled to that locale in search of his lost son. Mr. Steffan was unable to follow up on any reports as he did not have the means to travel.

Despite massive searches by an unprecedented number of participants, no sign was ever found of either the Adams or Steffan boy. After several months, the local communities returned to normal. The families of the boy's never did.

Several years after his son disappeared, a known swindler, Frank Barnes (*Volume II, Elk County Murders, The Infamous Skeleton*), freshly out of state prison, appeared at Mr. Steffan's door. Barnes had already visited Mr. Adams in Lamont and attempted to extort $25 to reveal the location of his missing son. Mr. Adams had refused and reported him to the local Kane Police Chief Ives. Barnes had meanwhile traveled to Ludlow and met up with Mr. Steffan, where he succeeded in getting the $25 from the poor laborer. Ives, knowing of the criminal past of Barnes, sent his deputies to Ludlow, and they immediately arrested Barnes, who they found walking the streets. He was placed in the lockup in Sheffield. When they searched him in Sheffield, he was found not to be carrying the $25 he received from Mr. Steffan nor the papers he had shown him, which identified the location of young Steffan. It was assumed that he threw out the money and papers on the way to the jail, or he burned them when asking for a match for his cigar. Barnes stated he was a private detective and did give the authorities the name of a gypsy camp in Ohio where the young boys were supposedly held. None of the tips panned out, and the boys were not found. Barnes was sent back to prison for the offense of obtaining money under false pretense, but he never gave up his life of crime.

The only other incident which brought the missing boys back into the limelight occurred in 1919 and came from, of all places, Italy. It seems a red cross nurse from Butler, Pa. was serving in Italy and had the chance to take care of a wounded American soldier. That soldier told her his name was Edwin Adams and that he had grown up near Kane, PA. The nurse remembered when young Edwin disappeared and wrote back to her parents of what she had been told. Her parents took the letter to the authorities who launched an investigation. The Adams were contacted, and with much anticipation, they awaited to hear if this almost impossible discovery was real. The Adam's also had a son, Homer, who was serving in France at that time, and he too began to look into the sighting. The parents of the Steffan boy were notified of this development and realizing their son would now be eighteen and subject to the draft, they reached out to the government to look into if their son was serving in the military. The Department of Defense notified the Steffans that no soldier with the name and age of Michael had entered the service of the nation during the great war. Another glimmer of hope was dashed. Unfortunately for the Adams family, the soldier who identified himself as "Edwin Adams" was never found, and it was thought that this was a cruel hoax perpetrated by someone familiar with the disappearance.

The Steffan family never gave up hope that their son would someday walk through their door and lived the rest of their lives on their farm on Main Street in Ludlow, very near the stream where their son disappeared from. Mr. Steffan was often observed walking along Windfall Run, perhaps hoping to find a clue that was missed all those years before. You can find Windfall Run right behind the Ludlow Post Office. Mr. Steffan died in 1940, and his wife followed in 1946. Both are buried in St. Michael's Byzantine Catholic Cemetery in Sheffield, Warren County.

What happened to Michael Steffan and Edwin Adams? The Adams boy was most certainly kidnapped for nefarious reasons and spirited out of the area. One can only imagine what happened to him after that, but he certainly was nowhere near Elk County after that day. Little Michael Steffan, while disappearing on the same day, was a little more complicated. No one witnessed a stranger in the area (*like the boys with Adams did*), and for these cases to be connected, it would have been almost impossible for the same person to kidnap Michael and then travel thirteen miles up the road and kidnap the Adam's boy. Was it perhaps two separate individuals that did these crimes? That is certainly a possibility. The two may have been connected, as these disappearances took place on the same day. If the Steffan boy was not kidnapped, it is possible that he wandered endlessly in the mountains by Ludlow and succumbed to the elements. In researching similar disappearances in which a body was eventually found, it was often fifteen to twenty miles away from where the child was last seen. The search parties concentrated on roughly four miles around Ludlow, so it is very possible his body was not discovered. I guess we will never know what happened to young Steffan, unless someday, somewhere, remains of a young boy are discovered in the mountains surrounding Ludlow.

Westline

The Western State Penitentiary booking photo of Guiseppe "Joseph" Ferraino.

Giuseppe (*Joe*) Ferraino appeared to have the American dream. He had immigrated from Italy in 1923 and had worked hard to become an American citizen and be able to bring his family over from Italy to join him. Joe had married in 1921 in Italy to Eleonora Zingrone, and the couple were soon blessed with a boy, Joe, Jr. Due to the economic collapse in Italy after the great war, work was scarce. Ferraino decided that the best way to support his family was to immigrate to the United States. Joe returned to Italy in 1926, and after the birth of a second child, a daughter Filomena, he returned to the States. Joe planned on gaining citizenship, and once he was a citizen, he would be able to apply for his family to come and join him. Joe did gain naturalization in 1930 but wanted to buy a property for his family to live in, and he scrimped to save money while also sending monthly payments to his wife in Italy. Joe had worked in Camden, New Jersey, Philadelphia, Sheffield, and Mayburg before finally settling in Westline, where he gained employment as a fireman at the Union Charcoal Company. Joe had saved $3,000 and used this money to purchase a small farm at Westline. He kept in contact with his wife through letters and the occasional phone call and promised her that the family would all be reunited in the future. Ferraino applied for visas for his family in November of 1937, but because of errors in the paperwork, the family was not able to immigrate until March of 1938. Joe had finally achieved what he had dreamed of since 1923. As his children and wife spoke no English, Joe had the children enrolled in the first grade at the Hamlin Township School in Westline on a fast track to learn English. The situation seemed perfect, but there would soon appear a conflict that would destroy this family forever.

On Wednesday, May 18th, 1938, Joe had finished his shift at the chemical plant and returned to his home. He spent an hour in the garden then went into the house. He secured a 16-gauge shotgun and told his son that he was going to go shoot a porcupine to eat. Joe Jr. was most interested in the pump shotgun as he had never seen one in Italy. Joe unloaded the shotgun and was wiping it down while Joe Jr. sat beside him, admiring the weapon. During this time, Mrs. Ferraino was cooking dinner and was walking back and forth in the kitchen, which was directly in front of the bench. Joe stood up from the bench and the shotgun fired. The round struck Mrs. Ferraino directly in the stomach at close range. Eleonora fell to the floor, mortally wounded, while her son and husband attempted to assist her to no avail. Ferraino ran to the neighbors for help and they called a doctor in Mt. Jewett and the authorities. Eleonora died almost instantly.

State Police Patrolman Andrew Hichenko arrived and after brief questioning, took Ferraino and his son into custody and transported them to the Kane barracks for a more thorough statement. Little Filomena was taken in by a neighboring family and had not witnessed the shooting. County Detective J. J. Allison and Sheriff Merle Dickinson joined Trooper Hichenko for the interrogation of Ferraino.

At the Kane substation, Ferraino gave his account of the shooting. He said he had returned home from work at the Union Charcoal Company at around 3 o'clock and then worked in his garden for about an hour. He said he spoke with his wife and son in the kitchen and then proposed to go into the woods to shoot a porcupine for them to eat. He brought out his 16-gauge pump shotgun, and his son expressed interest in the weapon, a type he had never seen before. Ferraino said he ejected four shells from the loaded weapon and said he forgot to eject the final and fifth round. He said he was showing the weapon to his son when he arose from the bench he was sitting on. As he rose, he said the gun had discharged, and the full load struck his wife in the abdomen from a distance of about three feet. He said his wife slumped to the floor and died before a Mt. Jewett physician arrived.

Joe Jr. told his story through an interpreter. Joey mentioned that there was another woman involved with his father, and he was suspicious. Joey told roughly the same story as his father with the exception that he said as his father held the shotgun, he glared at his wife and followed her movements in the kitchen with the barrel of the gun. Joey believed the shooting was intentional and was done because of the involvement of the other woman.

Ferraino was then questioned on having another woman, and he admitted that he had been out with other women while his wife was in Italy but denied caring for anyone in particular. Despite intense questioning, he never changed his story of how the shot was accidental and not planned. He was questioned until around 10:30 p.m. when he was taken by Trooper Hichenko and Sergeant John Mullaney to the Smethport jail to be held on suspicion of first-degree murder.

Ferraino and his son were taken back to their house the next day, May 19th, to reconstruct the shooting. Ironically, it was the two-month anniversary of when they had come to America, which was on March 19th. Both Ferrainos explained their versions of how the shooting happened, with the authorities playing the parts of Mrs. Ferraino and the father and son, respectively. Ferraino was once again steadfast in his claim that the shooting was an accident, while his son had added that he watched his father load his weapon with five shells but only ejected four. Young Ferraino also said that his father did not care for his mother but that they had not quarreled. Joey said he had remained in the kitchen with his mother since he returned home from school and was looking forward to hunting a porcupine with his father.

McKean County Deputy Coroner George Lull conducted an inquest over the body of Eleonora at the Lantz Funeral Home in Mt. Jewett. The only witness heard was Joe Jr., who reiterated his story and added that his father had been polishing the barrel of the weapon and followed his mother with the barrel as she walked back and forth, preparing dinner. The jury found that Eleonora Ferraino came to her death from a gunshot in the hands of Joseph Ferraino.

Ferraino was returned to the Smethport jail, and arrangements were made for a preliminary hearing on whether to charge him with the murder of his wife. Ferraino was formally arraigned in front of Justice of the Peace Gleason in Smethport on Thursday morning, May 21st, and the charges of murder in the first-degree were bound over to the criminal court for a formal trial to be held shortly.

The committal service for Mrs. Ferraino was held at the Lantz Funeral Home with the Reverend Alfred Bauer of the Saint Joseph Catholic Church in Mt. Jewett officiating. Burial took place in the Bridgeview Cemetery outside of Mt. Jewett, where her body still rests today. Eleonora was thirty-eight years of age when she met her death and was born in Catanzaro, Italy, to Dominic and Luace Ispozita Zingrone. She had only been in America for a little under two months.

The trial for Joseph Ferraino commenced in the Smethport Courthouse on July 11th with the selection of the jury. Those selected included J. B. Shea, William Nelson, Justine Fuller, Harland Fling, Mrs. Lyle Cook, Edward Booth, Peter Beal, Mrs. E. W. Fitzgerald, O. L. Shelgren, Frank White, Mrs. John Lonshore, and Roy Grandin. District Attorney Claude Shattuck, assisted by Smethport Attorney Robert Apple, represented the prosecution. Attorneys Joseph Wilson of Smethport and Henry Onofrio of Bradford represented the defense. Judge Charles Hubbard presided.

The prosecution presented that they would prove that *(Giuseppe)* Joseph Ferraino had murdered his wife as a result of a love triangle, and his motives were the fact that he loved another woman and that he had taken out an insurance policy right before the shooting. The one eyewitness to the shooting, Joe Jr., would testify that his father shot his mother deliberately.

State Trooper Andrew Hichenko was called first. He related how he arrived at the Ferraino home in Westline at around 5:50 p.m. on May 18th and found Mrs. Ferraino dead from a gunshot wound lying on the kitchen floor. Hichenko questioned Mr. Ferraino as to the whereabouts of the death gun, but Ferraino said he did not know. Later, when Hichenko found the shotgun in a closet in another room in the house, Ferraino admitted that this was the deadly weapon. Hichenko said the shotgun had one spent shell in its chamber.

County Detective Allison then testified. He told of going to Westline the day after the shooting to reenact the event. He said Ferraino first told him he was cleaning his gun with a white handkerchief before the accident. Allison then said Ferraino told him it was not a white handkerchief, but a blue one after Allison saw no dirt on the white one.

Joe Ferraino Jr. was then called. He testified that his father was showing him the shotgun in anticipation of going hunting for a porcupine. Joey said his father loaded the weapon with five shells but had ejected only four when he started to clean it. He said his father had begun to clean the weapon but followed his mother with the shotgun barrel while she walked back and forth, preparing dinner. Joey then said his father laid down the handkerchief and pointed the barrel at his mother and fired. When his mother fell to the floor, his dad had said to him, "I'm a ruined man."

The prosecution then identified Mrs. Alma Capasino of Sheffield as the woman that Joseph Ferraino had a love interest in. Love letters written by Capasino to Ferraino were discovered hidden in the Ferraino house during a search after the shooting.

Mrs. James Vincent of Sheffield stated that Ferraino had visited Mrs. Capasino many times at the latter's home.

Mrs. Teresa Stroup of Westline, who resides across the street from the Ferraino home, testified that Mrs. Capasino had visited Ferraino at his home on Mother's day, May 8th. She said Mrs. Ferraino was crying after Mrs. Capasino left her house.

Edward Harner of Westline and a fellow employee of Ferraino testified that Ferraino had introduced Capasino to him and said she was his sister–in–law.

Attorney Apple then introduced a life insurance policy into evidence. The policy Ferraino took out on his wife was for $2,000, and it had an accidental death benefit double that for $4,000. Ferraino had taken this policy out several weeks before the shooting and named himself as the beneficiary. The policy had become effective two days before the shooting. On cross-examination, the defense brought out that it was the agent and not Ferraino who brought up the addition of the accidental death clause.

Mrs. Alma Capasino was then called to the stand. She was shown a dozen love letters that had been written to Ferraino and which were discovered hidden in the Ferraino kitchen. Capasino admitted she did write the letters, but when asked to translate them, as they were written in Italian, she said she could not without the assistance of an Italian-English dictionary she had at her home. The prosecution brought in an interpreter who read all of the letters to the jury.

"My dear Love: Received your letter started with a kiss. When I pass the place where you lived, I have a pain in my heart. I'll not stay here now that you are not here. Come and give me a kiss. I love you, my dear. I send you one thousand kisses. Your wife, Alma."

"Mr. Joe: today is Sunday. My dear. I am suffering a lot for you. Last night I waited for you, and today I look for you. My dear, I'll always love you. When you see another woman, you'll forget me, and then I'll come at night and kill her. I am yours forever, and you are mine. Alma".

"Dear husband Joey, today I went to the post office expecting to see you. You know I love you a lot and my heart is beating hard. Come my love, so I can hold you in my arms and give you one thousand kisses. When you want me to stay at home, I think that you have another one that you have never told me about. Alma."

Mrs. Capasino explained she addressed Ferraino as dear husband merely in jest. She stated that she had visited at the Ferraino home on Mother's Day and that she had talked to Mrs. Ferraino. She said she explained her relations with Ferraino were only friendly. Alma said she and Mrs. Ferraino had parted on friendly terms.

Joseph Apa, of Olean, a cousin of Joseph Ferraino, furnished testimony that he had visited the Ferraino's three days before the fatal shooting. Apa had received a letter from Mrs. Ferraino requesting his assistance in breaking up the relationship between her husband and Mrs. Capasino. At that time, he remonstrated with his cousin concerning the letters reporting romance with Mrs. Capasino. Apa urged him to break off all relations with her and take care of his wife and children. Apa said that Ferraino had assured him he would, but it would have to be gradually and not immediate.

Frank Capasino, the husband of Alma, appeared as another witness for the prosecution and testified that he knew of several occasions when his wife and Ferraino had been together, ever since the accused had moved next door to them in Sheffield during the fall of 1936. He knew that Ferraino had been seen in the company of Mrs. Capasino and it was well known in Sheffield.

Urban Milton, a Westline resident, stated that he had acted as a driver for Mrs. Alma Capasino and Ferraino since Ferraino was not a licensed driver. Melton testified that he had driven for the couple three or four times, once on Mother's Day. He said he drove the two together on other occasions. Milton said that sometimes Joe sat in the front with him and other times in the back with Mrs. Capasino. He said the trips were from Westline to Warren, and they started six months ago. Milton stated that he sometimes brought the two to the Ferraino home but was unable to tell the court how long they stayed there or how she went back to Warren. He said he was not sure as he had not driven them back to Warren. When asked if anyone was at the Ferraino home when he dropped both of them off, he said no one. He never saw anyone else at the Ferraino home during these visits.

Joe jr. was called back to the stand and testified that when the gun exploded in his father's hands, the handkerchief that Ferraino was using to clean the gun was on the bench and no longer in his hand. He once again said that his father continually pointed the barrel of the gun in the direction of his mother as she moved about the kitchen, preparing food for them. This contradicted Ferraino's statement that he was cleaning the gun with his handkerchief when it accidentally went off.

Sheriff Merle Dickinson was called to the witness stand, and he disclosed the hiding place of Mrs. Capasino's love letters to the defendant, and he stated they were found in a small cubbyhole above the kitchen ceiling. Dickinson said that they were unnoticeable to anyone standing in the kitchen and could only be found by a tall person or someone with the help of a ladder. After several other witnesses testified as to the time of the shooting, the prosecution rested.

The defense began by calling the accused Joseph Ferraino to the stand. Ferraino testified that just before the gun went off, he had the handkerchief in his hand and was rubbing the gun with it near the trigger and that as he rose to his feet from a small bench on which he was sitting, the gun exploded. When questioned about the letters written to him by Mrs. Alma Capasino of Sheffield, he testified that he had taken the letters and photographs from his suitcase and put them in the kitchen ceiling because if they *(the authorities)* found them, they would have "fun with me." He also said that he had written to Mrs. Capasino once in a while, but he didn't know on what dates he wrote the letters. He testified that he had planned to have his wife come to this country from Italy in November of 1937, but there had been a mistake in the paperwork and that there was a delay until March when she came to Westline with his two children. Ferraino did not deny that he had told his cousin Apa that he would gradually break his "friendship" with Mrs. Capasino but reiterated that he meant the friendship as they were not lovers.

The prosecution, on cross-examination, attempted to break Ferraino's story of the shot being of an accidental nature. Ferraino clung to his story that this was nothing more than an accident and his testimony was not able to be broken.

On cross-examination, Ferraino told of planning for ten years to bring his family to this country from Italy contrary to the prosecution's attempts to show he was not anyway interested in having his wife's arrival break up his friendship with Mrs. Alma Capasino. He told of buying a farm for his wife and kids with $3000 he had saved up in this country. He explained he was not an American citizen in 1927 and could not bring his family with him when he returned to the United States. He stated that when he returned to the United States, he immediately took out his first naturalization papers and became a citizen in 1930. Ferraino stated that on the day of the shooting, he had returned from work shortly after 3:00 p.m., and after being met by his wife, he went out to his garden where he worked for more than an hour. He stated that he came into the house, changed clothes, and at his wife's request, went down to the Buffington store to purchase some pepper. Outside the store, he stated that he talked shortly with Margaret Buffington and then went inside, where he purchased the pepper from Mary Patrick. Shortly after 4:30, he returned home to his wife and went into the dining room where he picked up his gun and five shells. His wife Eleonora came into the room and sat down beside the stove, and his sixteen-year-old son Joe Jr. and his daughter also came in and stood on his right side in the doorway. After his son's request to demonstrate to him how the gun worked, Ferraino loaded the gun and then withdrew the shells for the sons' benefit. Joe Jr. picked up some of the shells and started pounding them on the floor, an act for which the father scolded him. The defendant testified that the entire time the barrel of the gun had been pointing towards the doorway away from the son and that Mrs. Ferraino was not in the line of fire. He demonstrated before the court his actions while showing off the gun to his family, explaining how he cradled the firearm in his lap. He stated that immediately after scolding his son for the misuse of the shells, his wife suggested that he put up the gun and come to supper. Mrs. Ferraino moved towards the doorway in which direction the gun was pointed and as he arose the gun exploded. He next noticed his wife lying in a crumpled heap on the floor. Dropping the gun, he raced to his wife's side, and after calling to her for a few seconds, he went outside to summon help.

Ferraino went on to explain his relationship with Mrs. Alma Capasino of Sheffield. Joe testified that he first met Mrs. Capasino in April of 1936. "When I sent for my wife, I talked with Alma and told her that once my woman came, I did not want to have anything more to do with her. She said, "OK." She even took me to Olean to get a lawyer to make out papers to bring my woman over to this country. After my woman was in the country, Mrs. Capasino came to my house three times. Once with friends, once on May 8th, and once after that. Mrs. Capasino told my wife "I am not trying to steal your man," and my wife told her that she was not mad and told her to come to her house anytime she wanted to come. My wife offered her a cup of coffee and said she didn't pay any attention to the talk of the neighbors." Ferraino stated he never quarreled with his wife. In answer to the question about how he and his wife got along, he answered, "pretty good."

On the question of the insurance policy, Ferraino explained that in 1933 he went to Olean and took a life insurance policy on himself for $1000 and made his wife and children the beneficiaries. This policy had a double indemnity clause where it would pay double if the death was accidental. He sent the premium each month to Olean by money order. When he thought of buying insurance for his wife, he had his friends call the Prudential man in Mt. Jewett. He preferred this because the agent came to the house and collected the money, and he would not have to purchase a money order or stamp to send in his payment.

The defense stated in their closing argument that Ferraino had accidentally shot his wife, and this was a tragic accident and nothing else. They argued the insurance policy as a motive was discredited and that the testimony of Joe Jr. was as a result of Ferraino having corrected Joe Jr. and that he was angry at this father. The relationship with Mrs. Capasino was nothing more than a close friendship, which was not romantic and, in fact, was waning before the accident happened.

The prosecution argued that the shooting was nothing more than cold-blooded murder. The murder took place because Ferraino wanted to continue his relationship with Mrs. Capasino and the insurance policy was the second motive. The fact that his only son had contradicted his account of the shooting cemented these motives.

Judge Hubbard then took charge of the case and presented the following charge to the jury: "You remember how Joe Jr. who was at the scene in the little home at Westline testified how his father was cleaning the gun....You will remember how the son testified that the defendant followed her (*Mrs. Ferraino*) around the kitchen with the gun for over an hour. "

"The defendant gives a very different story saying that he was cleaning the gun for only a short period.... You will also recall how he (*Ferraino*) went into the garden when he came home from work at 3:00 p.m. He stated that he worked for about an hour and twenty minutes then went into the house, changed his suit and went to Buffington's store, came back between 4:30 p.m. and 5:00 p.m., picked up his pump-action shotgun and started cleaning it off before going porcupine hunting. He testified that his son asked him how the gun worked.... the defendant said that he thought the gun was empty, and when he got up, the gun went off accidentally, so he testifies."

"These two points are both important ones. It is up to you, the jury, to decide which one is true when it is apparent that one is lying or very much mistaken, you must pay particular attention to the statements."

"You will also remember the son's testimony as to the handkerchief which it is alleged Ferraino was cleaning the gun with, falling on the bench and that young Joe saw it drop three or four minutes before the shooting.... The father said that the gun and the handkerchief dropped at the same time when the gun went off."

"It is for you to decide which is right. Did the son see his father drop the handkerchief three or four minutes before the gun went off, or did he assume that?"

"Much of the time was taken up to find a motive. One was the insurance policy that was taken out in March 1938 and went into effect about a week before the shooting. You will recall in the insurance agent's testimony that it was he who suggested the double indemnity policy. The defendant was named as beneficiary."

"The second point of the testimony alleged to show motives was the relations of the defendant with Mrs. Alma Capasino. You heard the letters offered. Some of the letters suggestive of a great feeling of intimacy towards each other. You will recall that she referred in one or two of her letters to a promise that the defendant is supposed to have made."

"All the testimony was brought out to show a motive for the defendant's killing of his wife."

"You will remember Joe Apa's testimony (*Ferraino's first cousin*) in telling Ferraino to keep off of Alma Capasino and the defendant's reaction saying he would break off gradually."

"The defendant said that he and his wife never quarreled over Alma, but in a letter that Mrs. Ferraino wrote to Joe's cousin Apa in Olean, N.Y., she stated that she knew of the affair between Alma and Joe."

"You will also remember how a nearby neighbor said she saw Mrs. Ferraino cry when Alma visited Joe on Mother's Day in Westline."

"Is the defendant telling the truth when he says his wife did not mind his associating with Mrs. Capasino?"

Defense Attorney Wilson then presented the closing remarks to the jury. Wilson reiterated the testimony of the defendant going to great lengths to impress upon the jury the actions with the gun in front of his woman could have brought about accidental death and nothing else. Attorney Wilson asked the jury why, if the defendant Joe Ferraino had chosen to his to kill his wife willfully, had he picked a time when the son and daughter were in the room watching him. Attorney Wilson brought out the point that the defendant's association with Alma Capasino was not to be denied. Still, he pointed out those associations were severed following a letter written by her to the defendant in which she told him to stay with who he loved, admitting her removal from his life.

District Attorney Shattuck then took the floor and in a capable manner pointed out that the testimony of Joseph Ferraino Jr., an eyewitness to the shooting, and the series of love letters written by Mrs. Capasino, the other woman in the case, and the insurance policy as the motives for the actual crime. Attorney Shattuck read a letter identified as one sent by the deceased woman to a cousin Ralph Apa, asking for influence in breaking up her husband's relationship with Mrs. Capasino. She closed her letter with the statement that she was ashamed of his marshaling two wives with one husband. The prosecutor pointed out errors in Ferraino's testimony; he said the defendant claimed that his son and daughter were in the room at the time of the so-called accident, whereby evidence proves that no one but Joe Jr. was in the same room at the time. The daughter said that she had gone to the bathroom and was in there when she heard the shot. Shattuck closed his address with the statement: "For God's sakes bring in the true verdict!" The judge then instructed the jurors to retire to reach a verdict.

The jury left the courtroom at 11:00 a.m. on July 19th and took nearly four and a half hours to reach a verdict at 3:42 in the afternoon. They returned the verdict of "guilty of murder in the first-degree," and they recommended life imprisonment. Ferraino's defense attorneys immediately made a verbal motion for a new trial. Judge Hubbard notified them that a written motion for a new trial needed to be filed by 10:00 a.m. the next Monday morning to be considered. Ferraino showed no emotion at his guilty verdict but was noticed to look at the jury in complete amazement. He was returned to the county jail.

The defense attorneys were unsuccessful in their attempt to seek a new trial, and Ferraino was transferred to the Western Penitentiary on July 28th, 1938, to serve out his life sentence. Over the years, Ferraino applied for a pardon, and this was continuously denied. Ferraino did eventually end up being released early from his life sentence and spent his final days in Pittsburgh. Ferraino died in Pittsburgh on August 27th, 1967 and was buried in the Hollywood Memorial Park Cemetery within the city limits. Joe Jr. ended up in the Erie Children's Home, where he lived until he was age eighteen and Joe's daughter Philomena went to live with relatives in Olean.

The grave of Eleonora in Bridgeview Cemetery.

In Defense of Her Honor

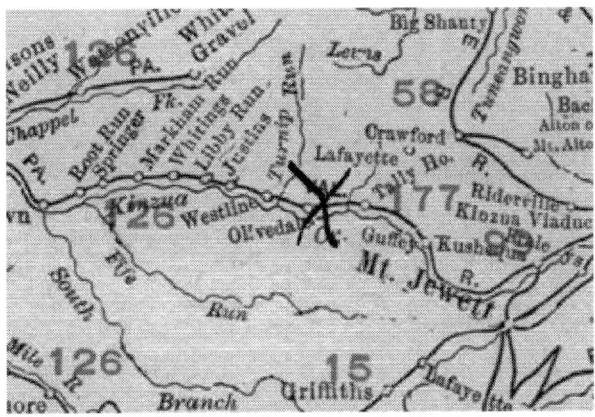

A map showing where the ghostown of Olivedale once existed.

Olivedale was a small settlement located two miles east of today's Westline. The livelihood in this small village was a chemical plant that produced charcoal. The Gaffney Brothers of Bradford had built this plant, among others, and the plant was surrounded by five company houses for the workers. The only reason people lived in these tiny towns was usually employment at the factory. A common practice to earn extra money in these company houses was to rent a spare room to single men. The landlords welcomed the extra income as times were always tough during this era.

One of these company houses was occupied by Mr. Edward and Mrs. May Burdick in 1902. Mr. Burdick was employed at the Gaffney plant, and May was a housekeeper. They rented a room to a Mr. John Ryan, a young worker who had recently arrived in Olivedale and who was employed as a laborer in the surrounding lumber concerns. Ryan, hailing from the Philadelphia area, was around thirty years old. He stood over six feet tall and weighed over two hundred pounds. In addition to providing lodging, the agreement with Ryan was that all meals were also included. May happily cooked meals for all three occupants of the house. In the last few days before Christmas, Ryan acquired several bottles of liquor to celebrate, and on the evening of December 22nd, he apparently celebrated a little too much. On Wednesday morning, December 23rd, Ryan did not show up in the kitchen, as was his custom for breakfast before heading out to his job. Mrs. Burdick attempted to rouse Ryan from his room, but her knocks went unanswered. May continued about her daily routine of cleaning and decorating for the holidays and prepared lunch for her husband and her tenant, expecting Ryan to join them. Mr. Burdick returned each day from the nearby plant for lunch, but once again, Ryan did not leave his room to join them. The Burdick's discussed Ryan's absence, and soon Mr. Burdick had to return to his job. May kept Ryan's portion warm and went up the stairs to attempt to rouse him once again. Receiving no reply, she went about her daily cleaning routine, and while in the front parlor, she tried the side door and found it locked. She thought this peculiar and then headed towards the kitchen door, which was the only other means of escape from the house. As she turned to go into the kitchen, she was immediately seized by Ryan, who grabbed her by the wrists and blocked her path to the kitchen door. Ryan also began to tell May how he was going to molest her and how much he had waited for this moment. May, a beautiful woman who barely weighed one hundred pounds, realized she would be no match for Ryan, and through a strenuous effort, she managed to break free from Ryan's grasp and quickly ran up the stairs to her bedroom. May knew there were several guns in the room and that if she was quick enough, she could lock Ryan out of the room and safely gather up a gun. As she ran up the stairs, she screamed for help, but as there were no near neighbors of the Burdick's, no one heard her. May reached her bedroom door and ran in and attempted to close it but was quickly followed by Ryan, who blocked her attempts. She grabbed a shotgun that was behind the door, and feebly attempted to point it at Ryan, but he quickly gained control of the gun and pushed the muzzle aside. He then grabbed her by the throat and pushed her onto the bed. May struggled with all her might, but Ryan was able to remove her lower clothing and began to molest her. As the assault continued, she remembered that her husband kept a loaded pistol beside her bed on a chair, and with great difficulty, she seized the weapon and pointed it at the head of her rapist. She told Ryan that if he did not stop, she would shoot. Ryan continued his assault and laughed at her. She repeated her threat several times, and when Ryan did not stop, she placed the muzzle against his left side and fired. Ryan immediately rolled off of her and onto the floor. May did not check to see if he was dead but put her clothes on in a hurry and rushed to the neighbor's house for help.

Mrs. Burdick headed to the Norcross residence, which was across the street. She rushed into the house and was met by Mrs. Norcross, who was in the kitchen. Mrs. Norcross stood in amazement as May reported the attack and subsequent shooting. Burdick, blood-spattered on her face, neck, and clothes and hair disheveled, presented a horrific site compared to her usual appearance, which was always of the best taste. May asked her neighbor to please go and get her husband at the plant and tell him what had happened. Norcross, frozen by the sudden interruption of her day did not move; May ran out in front of the house and caught a young boy walking down the street. She sent him to locate her husband.

Several other neighbors then joined May as she went back into her residence to check on Ryan. They found Ryan lying on the floor of his bedroom near the door. The sheets on his bed had streaks of blood on them. It appeared he had fallen face-first onto it and had slid onto the floor. May told the neighbors that she had shot him when he was on her bed, and he must not have died and stumbled into his room while she was across the street at Norcross's. Word was sent for Coroner Dr. B. H. Hall to come to Olivedale to investigate the matter.

Coroner Hall traveled from Bradford and hastily conducted a coroner's inquest. Hall took the testimony of Burdick, her neighbors, and others who had witnessed the scene of the shooting. An examination of the body of Ryan found that a bullet had entered his left side and passed through his heart, causing almost instantaneous death.

The inquest then adjourned to await a formal autopsy of Ryan and all collaborating witness statements. The coroner's jury met again the next day and found that Ryan had met his death at the hands of a bullet fired by Mrs. May Burdick. The jury also recommended that no charges be filed as they believed this was a case of self-defense.

District Attorney Melvin studied the case and the findings of the coroner's inquest and believed that the case was not an outright case of self-defense, this being because several discrepancies had been uncovered during and after the inquest. Melvin decided he would pursue a grand jury on the matter and sent Constable Harrington to Olivedale with a warrant for the arrest of Mrs. Burdick on the charge of murder in the death of John Ryan. Harrington found that Mrs. Burdick was not in Olivedale but away on a visit. Mr. Burdick promised Harrington that he would go and bring her for questioning in the matter, and Harrington left. The Burdicks went to Bradford together and checked into the Oil City House for a stay while the warrant was resolved. Mrs. Burdick again stated her case to District Attorney Melvin, and partially due to her demeanor in not being opposed to a trial; she was released back to the hotel on her own recognizance, pending a hearing in front of Judge Bouton in the McKean County Court. On Monday, January 2nd, 1903, a habeas corpus hearing was held in front of Judge Bouton in the Smethport Courthouse. Mrs. Burdick repeated her story of the shooting, and the Judge opinioned that this was a bailable case, and he set the amount at $2,000. Mr. Harry Gaffey, employer of Mr. Burdick, put up this amount and also stated he would be helping fund the defense. Judge Bouton then allowed Mrs. Burdick to leave the courthouse on bail pending a grand jury, which would be scheduled in February.

The grand jury convened in Smethport on February 24th. Judge Bouton presided while Assistant District Attorney Eugene Mullin represented the Commonwealth and Attorney John Mullin represented the defendant.

Eugene Mullin opened the case for the Commonwealth by calling Mrs. Norcross as his first witness. Norcross stated that on the afternoon of December 23rd, Mrs. Burdick came to her house with blood on her face and neck, looking quite disheveled. She said Mrs. Burdick asked her to get Mr. Burdick from work and that she had shot John Ryan. Mrs. Norcross said she did not go, but a passing boy did go to get Mr. Burdick. Norcross repeated the story that Mrs. Burdick had told her about the shooting. She also mentioned that on the following day, Mrs. Burdick had added that Ryan had forced her to submit to his wishes in the morning and that Ryan had tried again in the afternoon and that is when she shot him.

Several witnesses were called to testify as to what they saw when they entered the Burdick residence. All testified that they found the body of Ryan lying on the floor in his bedroom and that it looked like he had fallen face first onto his bed, and his body had slid onto the floor, leaving a trail of blood. The only blood they saw was coming from Ryan's nose and mouth.

Dr. B. H. Hall, the coroner, testified that the wound which caused Ryan's death was made by a bullet from a revolver; that the revolver had been held very close to Ryan's body, as the coat he wore was badly burned by powder. He also said that the course of the bullet showed that the revolver had been pointing downward slightly when fired.

Mrs. Daily, a neighbor of the accused, testified next. She said that Mrs. Burdick had told her the next morning that she had shot Ryan while he was in the hall between her bedroom and his own; and that two weeks later she told her he was in her bedroom.

Mr. and Mrs. Lawrence Black then testified. They were the first people present in the Burdick house after the shooting. They testified as to seeing the body of Ryan lying on his bedroom floor and described Mrs. Burdick as having blood on her face, her clothing disheveled, and that there were clear marks of violence upon her neck. The prosecution then rested.

Attorney John Mullin opened the defense by calling Mrs. Burdick to the stand. She stated that on the morning of December 23rd, Ryan, who had been boarding at her house for two weeks, was too drunk to go to work. She said that while she and her husband were eating their lunch, Ryan was lying in a stupor in his bedroom. She stated that when they finished their lunch, she went upstairs and heard Ryan moving about in his room. She went downstairs again to get Ryan his lunch. As she was downstairs, she said Ryan seized her and finding the downstairs escape routes locked, she ran upstairs and into her room with Ryan following closely. She picked up a shotgun and told him she would shoot him if he did not leave. He knocked it from her hands and then succeeded in his purpose to rape her. She said while she was being raped on her bed, she managed to grab a pistol that was kept on a chair near the bed and placed it beside Ryan's head, and threatened to shoot him. She said Ryan then began to choke her, and she put the revolver to his side and pulled the trigger. She said she immediately ran from the room and to Mrs. Norcross's house for help. She vehemently denied ever telling Mrs. Norcross or Mrs. Daily any of the stories which they testified to.

Mullin called Mrs. Norcross and Mrs. Black back to the stand, and they both testified that there were black and blue marks on Mrs. Burdick's neck and that her clothing and hair were disheveled. They both also stated that the marks on her neck were not visible the next day.

Mr. Burdick and several other people then testified that the story Mrs. Burdick had told on the stand was the same story she had told them on day one and that her story never changed. The defense then rested.

After the prosecution and defense presented their closing arguments, Judge Bouton charged the jury to carefully consider the evidence and the testimony. The jury returned after two hours and found Mrs. Burdick not guilty, and she was discharged from the court. One could wonder why the district attorney pursued charges in the first place in this case. Although there were some discrepancies, such as Mrs. Burdick telling variations of the assault and whether it had happened previously, it was pretty clear that the shooting of Ryan was justified.

An interesting aftermath to this case occurred five years later when the Burdicks had moved to Lewis Run as Mr. Burdick had gained employment at the chemical factory there. One day in September of 1907, while her husband was at work, Mrs. Burdick took a .32 caliber pistol and aimed it at her left breast and fired. Her purpose seemed to be to hit her heart and cause her death. Her aim was not accurate, and the bullet took a downward course passing through her stomach. Mrs. Burdick was not expected to survive and speculation at that time was that this suicide attempt had something to do with the death of Ryan five years previous. The doctors did not attempt to remove the bullet as it was considered a fatal shot that would end in the woman's death. Mrs. Burdick was asked why she had attempted to end her life, and she replied that she did not know why she had shot herself. Her husband stated that he saw nothing in her manner or conduct to suggest she was about to put an end to her existence, and all involved could come up with no explanation.

Mrs. Burdick miraculously survived this usually fatal wound and continued to live in Lewis Run. She never explained why she had attempted suicide, and she took the secret to her grave. May did end up dying young, however, from cellulitis and general neuritis in 1913. This cause of death was possibly from complications from the earlier suicide attempt. She never had children and is buried in the Degolia Cemetery. I often wonder if there was more to this story, but we will never know. When John Ryan's body was found, he had his pants and all of his clothes on; if he was sexually assaulting Mrs. Burdick, one would think he would have disrobed. I could not find any information on what happened to the body of John Ryan, and it can only be speculated that the body was buried in a pauper's grave somewhere near Olivedale.

ACKNOWLEDGMENTS

I would like to thank Mrs. Laura Isadore, McKean County Prothonotary for providing me access to all the criminal records I used in my research. Many of the cases were supplemented by news accounts produced by long deceased reporters from The Bradford Era, The Kane Republican, The McKean Miner and other excellent newspapers which are no longer published. Thanks also to my many loyal readers who have given me so much positive feedback and encouragement. Appreciation also to my family and friends who have supported me in this often-exhaustive research and writing which takes away time with them. All illustrations in this book are either in the public domain or the property of the author unless otherwise noted.

OTHER FINE BOOKS AVAILABLE FROM BAUMGRATZ PUBLISHING, LLC

elkcountymurder.com
mckeancountymurder.com

- *Tiger at the Bar, The Life Story of Charles Margiotti* by Chester Harris
- *Elk County, A Journey through time* by John Imhof
- *Gettysburg Day 2, A study in Maps* by John Imhof
- *History of Capital Crimes, Confessions and Death Penalties in Clearfield County 1816 – 1914*
- *Greater Pittsburgers As We See Them* 1906
- *Elk County Murders Volume I*
- *Elk County Murders Volume II*
- *Elk County Murders Volume III*
- *McKean County Murders Volume I*

Like us on Facebook!
Elkcountymurder.com
McKeancountymurder.com

Order Form

Please send Check or Money Order to:

Baumgratz Publishing, LLC
P.O. Box 100
Ridgway, PA 15853

Title	Cost Each	Total
Elk County Murders Volume I	$24.95	_____
Elk County Murders Volume II	$24.95	_____
Elk County Murders Volume III	$24.95	_____
Tiger at the Bar	$42.95	_____
Elk County Journey Through Time	$24.95	_____
History of Capital Crimes, Clearfield	$8.95	_____
McKean County Murders Volume I	$24.95	_____
Shipping and Handling:		$3.99
Total Enclosed:	$	_____

Please enclose your name, address, and email address.

Thank You for Your Order!